£1

A TIME TO CARE

A Time to Care

Mildmay's Response to People with AIDS

Ruth Sims

Hodder & Stoughton
LONDON SYDNEY AUCKLAND

Copyright © 1996 by Ruth Sims

First published in Great Britain 1996

The right of Ruth Sims to be identified as the Author of
the Work has been asserted by her in accordance with the
Copyright, Designs and Patents Act 1988.

10 9 8 7 6 5 4 3 2 1

British Library Cataloguing in Publication Data
A record for this book is available from the British Library

ISBN 0 340 66148 8

Printed and bound in Great Britain by

Cox & Wyman Ltd, Reading, Berks

Hodder and Stoughton Ltd
A Division of Hodder Headline PLC
338 Euston Road
London NW1 3BH

There is a time for
everything,
and a season for every activity
under heaven.
(Ecc. 3:1)

ACKNOWLEDGMENTS

Many people have helped and encouraged me in the writing of this book and I should like them to know how much their encouragement and support has been appreciated.

HRH the Princess of Wales her interest and for writing the Foreword for the book.

The President, Chairman of the Board of Trustees and staff of Mildmay Mission Hospital and especially my colleagues on the executive directorate.

Dr Veronica Moss, now Director/Medical of Mildmay UK, who gave so much time to working with me on the first editing and who assisted me so many ways.

Mr Derek Thompson for extracts from his book, *The Birth and Rebirth of a Unique Hospital*, published in 1992, about the history of Mildmay, which have been used in the Introduction of this book.

Miss Claire Wheatcroft, Communications Manager at Mildmay, for information derived from her publications, *Highlights*, Mildmay's newsletter.

Mrs Pauline Hamilton, Mrs Margaret Hyde and my house group, who supported me with their prayers whenever I was working on the book.

Sally-Anne, Nicky, Peter and David, my family, who encouraged and supported me throughout.

Mrs Bryony Benier, whose editing expertise has made this book what it is.

Finally, I must thank Mrs Dorothy Hannan, my personal assistant, for her patience, constant encouragement, and the hard work involved in preparing the manuscript and coping with numerous amendments.

CONTENTS

Acknowledgments vi

Foreword ix

An introduction to Mildmay xi

1 A time to prepare – 1987 1

2 A time of conflict and new understanding – 1987–8 19

3 A time of new beginnings – 1988 32

4 A time of growth – 1989 48

5 A time to pause and a time to reflect – 1990 61

6 A time to make changes – 1991 77

7 A time to be creative – 1991 91

8 A time to celebrate – 1992 102

9 A time of thanksgiving – 1992 117

10 A time to pull down and a time to build – 1993 133

11 A time of new opportunities – 1993–4 148

12 A time for more miracles – 1995 166

FOREWORD
by HRH the Princess of Wales

KENSINGTON PALACE

My first visit to Mildmay was on 24th February 1989 on the occasion of the first birthday of the remarkable AIDS hospice in London.

Since that time I have come to admire Mildmay as a place of comfort which cares not only for physical needs but also for emotional and spiritual relief. This book illustrates so well how Mildmay has found a time to care for those with AIDS whose expectations are as great as any with lives to lead. Single people, couples, mothers and their children, families ..... none is too much trouble for the staff who, like their charges, require the love and support of us all.

The stories you will find in this book are profoundly moving and will be a source of great strength and inspiration to everyone.

Diana .

February, 1996

AN INTRODUCTION
TO MILDMAY

How it all began

The name 'Mildmay' is derived from the work carried out in Mildmay Park, North London, by the Rev. William Pennefather. He was vicar of St Jude's, Mildmay Park, from 1864 to 1873 and developed from there a number of projects addressing spiritual and social needs. These were known collectively as the Mildmay institutions. Key players in the work of all the institutions were the Mildmay deaconesses, who were trained by Mrs Pennefather to 'heal the sick and preach the gospel'.

In 1866 there was an outbreak of cholera in East London. Two of the Mildmay deaconesses were working at that time in the ten-bed cottage hospital in nearby Islington. They volunteered to go to East London and care for people with cholera, along with the children and dependants of those who had already died.

Their work was based in a miserable alley called Cabbage Court in Bethnal Green. A leading daily paper described life in Bethnal Green in the 1860s in the following words:

It consists of a network of narrow streets – or rather passages, for the widest of these thoroughfares is only 28 ft; the ground floors in most cases lie below the level of the street and consist of the bare soil plus the impurities with which it has been saturated. Altogether 5,700 persons live their wretched lives in this doleful region, the average number of occupants to each room being 2.5. The rooms are very small . . . 15 acres of pollution boast 12 public houses, the only attractive places you see in the slums; they can afford fine glass windows, plenty of warmth and a welcome to all who come with their last penny though the babes are starving. The sign reads 'Drunk for a penny or dead drunk for threepence'.

It was into these foul streets, which even the police feared to enter, that the Mildmay deaconesses came to care for the cholera victims, the 'untouchables' of that time. Others were frightened to care for them and they were shunned due to fear and ignorance. Perhaps it is not surprising that the deaconesses were criticised by some Christians who thought that the work was not suitable for ladies!

The Hospital

The work of the deaconesses developed and expanded, and eight years later a local dispensary and an outpatient consulting room were opened. These were followed three years later by the first Mission Hospital, sited in a disused warehouse. It consisted of twenty-seven beds in three wards (for men, women and children) and the staff were made up of one doctor, three nurses and five deaconesses in training.

In 1892 Mildmay Mission Hospital opened on its present site and for many years it served as a charitable foundation responding to the medical, spiritual and social needs of the social community. Although it became part of the National Health Service in 1948, Mildmay was allowed to retain its Christian character and associations, in accordance with the 1946 Act of Parliament. Clause 61 of that Act states 'Where the character and association of any voluntary hospital transferred to the Minister by virtue of this Act are such as to link it with a particular religious denomination, regard shall be had in the general administration of the hospital and in the making of appointments to the Hospital Management Committee to the preservation of the character and association of the hospital.'

A new extension was added to the hospital in 1965, but despite this, as small hospitals with less than 200 beds were considered to be uneconomic, Mildmay Mission Hospital was closed down in 1982.

Down, but not out!

Undeterred, Mildmay and its supporters immediately began to investigate ways to overcome this blow. The fact that it did turn out to have a future is due largely to the unswerving loyalty and generosity of many Christians and local people, among whom Mildmay continues to be highly respected. The chief driving force behind the reopening of the hospital was the Mildmay Hospital Advisory Committee (HAC) under the chairmanship of Mrs Helen Taylor Thompson. Her vision and dedication played a vital role in the battle for Mildmay, and in subsequent developments. Her involvement in Mildmay stretched as far back as 1952, when she was invited to become a member of the Hospital Management Committee. She had always been a determined, unstoppable lady, with great faith. During the Second World War she had served with the Field Assisted Nursing Yeomanry in France and later became involved in coding operations and broadcasting to agents. Following a successful period in business at managing director and chairman level, she had decided to channel her considerable energies into the Health Service and charitable sector.

On 12 February 1984 the Minister of Health approved, in spite of an appeal, the decision taken eight months earlier by the District Health Authority to make closure of Mildmay permanent. The reason it took so long was that the Mildmay supporters had protested and launched an appeal, conducted a feasibility study to reopen Mildmay within the NHS, etc. – all of which were finally rejected by that decision on 12 February 1984.

In May 1984 the Minister issued approval for Mildmay to reopen, on the understanding that the hospital should benefit the local community and be financially viable. Thanks to the continued power of prayer and the generosity of benefactors, Mildmay was able to reopen in October 1985.

Recovering the vision

After nearly forty years, Mildmay was to revert to its status as
a voluntary Christian charitable hospital and could now seek to
recover the vision of its founders and apply this with a freedom
that would have been impossible had it remained within the
NHS. The Mildmay HAC was discontinued, to be replaced by
a Board of Governors with Mrs Taylor Thompson as its
Chairman.

One of the most significant moves made in the next twelve
months was the appointment of a Medical Director as the
executive head of Mildmay, who would lead the work to
identify the most necessary and appropriate services that Mildmay should provide. It was Mrs Helen Taylor Thompson's
suggestion that this appointment be made and, following consultation with the Board, she approached Dr Veronica Moss to
offer her the post. Dr Moss was a partner in a GP practice at
the time. She had considerable medical and missionary experience in India and had been Medical Advisor to the Church
Missionary Society as well as a member of Mildmay's HAC.
She was appointed to the post with effect from October 1986. I
joined Dr Moss six months later and that is where our story
begins.

1
A TIME TO PREPARE
1987

My move to Mildmay

The sun was shining brightly on that Sunday morning in January 1987. The tide was high and the waves were crashing up against the sea wall. There were a few couples walking along the promenade, mostly elderly, with their warm winter coats buttoned up and hats pulled well down to protect them against the strong wind. I was driving home from church along the sea front, enjoying the view, when suddenly I thought, 'I wonder what's happening at Mildmay'.

A few months earlier I had seen an advertisement in the *Nursing Times* for a Nursing Officer for the newly reopened Mildmay Mission Hospital, now a small community hospital with a remit to develop services which would benefit the local community in East London. The services they currently undertook were the care of young chronically sick and disabled people and provision for respite and convalescent beds for GP patients.

I had rung Mildmay about the post and had been told that it was residential and was given the figure for the salary. I could not take a residential post and anyway I had been put off by the man who had spoken to me as he seemed very gruff and disinterested. I did nothing more about the job. Here I was, however, on that wintry day three months later, wondering what had happened. I had quite an interest in Mildmay, because I had done my nursing training there and at the London Hospital, at a time when Mildmay was a small District General Hospital. As I drove along I thought: if only that post had been non-residential and the salary had been higher, I would have been interested. But I had a mortgage to pay and commuting to London would have been too expensive.

When I reached home I sat down to catch up on my reading. Amongst the journals were the last three copies of the *Nursing Times*. I glanced through them and read articles of interest and then moved on to the job advertisements as I always did. To my amazement there was an advertisement for a Matron for Mildmay Mission Hospital – at an increased salary and the post was non-residential! I had one immediate problem: this was an old journal and the closing date for applications was in four days' time. I felt compelled to make further enquiries, although I really could not understand why I was so interested. I loved my work in Southend, there would be the commuting, and besides, I had for many years had a special interest in terminal care for patients being cared for in their own homes. This had resulted in a scholarship and I had written a booklet on the subject for the Royal College of Nursing. This new work at Mildmay seemed to have no relevance to all that.

I prayed for guidance nonetheless, and the next day I rang Mildmay to ask if I could talk to somebody about the post before deciding whether to apply. I was given the opportunity to go to Mildmay the very next morning to meet informally with the Medical Director.

Arriving early the next day, I had a look around the area that had been so familiar to me twenty years before. Austin Street was still cobbled, which made it difficult to walk on with my best high-heeled shoes. I picked my way along to the gardens of St Leonard's Church (of 'Oranges and Lemons' fame), which were looking bleak and bare with the trees bereft of their leaves. The scene had not changed much. Homeless people wearing layers of clothes sat on the benches drinking and chatting, and on this chilly morning they were huddled together, their breath misting in the cold morning air.

The entrance to the hospital had now been moved, but I just had to walk up to the old door. I could remember so clearly the time when I had first been there. I was seventeen years old at the time, and I remembered listening to the first chime of the hospital clock as I went nervously through the doors for my interview for training. The sycamore tree which had been planted nearly a hundred years before was still flourishing, but the old clock, although still there, was not working.

Ten minutes before the appointed time, I walked into the new entrance of the hospital in Hackney Road and presented myself at the reception desk. The reception area was shabby, albeit comfortable, and my initial feeling of apprehension was deepening. 'What am I doing here?' I thought to myself. These feelings were compounded when an elderly, eccentric-looking lady with marcel waving and a hair slide walked across to a room off the reception area. 'She's bound to be the Medical Director,' I thought. 'This is absolute madness.' Just as I was about to pick up my briefcase and leave, a secretary came out and smiled at me. She had a cup of coffee in her hand which she offered to me with the words, 'Are you Mrs Sims? We're expecting you. Dr Moss will see you in just a moment.' As I sat drinking my coffee I reminded myself that the reason I was here was because I believed God had wanted me to come. Although I was something of a reluctant applicant, I knew I had to stay and see it through.

Then a door opened and a tall, elegant young woman came out, introduced herself as the Medical Director and invited me into her room. She did not have marcel waving and was not wearing a hair slide – what a relief! What she was about to tell me made sense of all my confusion and presented me, I believe, with what turned out to be the most exciting opportunity of my life.

God's plan

'At midnight last night,' she said, 'The Board of Mildmay unanimously agreed that a hospice for people with AIDS should be part of our services.' I couldn't believe what I was hearing.

'Caring for people with AIDS – how exciting! What a challenge!' Just how much of a challenge I had yet to find out. I had walked into that building not really wanting the job, but I came out desperately hoping that it was part of God's plan that I would be appointed.

As I left the Medical Director's office I was told that the present Matron would like to say 'hello' to me. Not only did I meet the Matron, but I also spoke with Mrs Taylor Thompson, the Chairman of the Board of Governors. We had a chat together over a cup of coffee and they asked me why I was interested in the post. 'I just think God is behind all this,' I replied, 'and I have just heard from Dr Moss that you're going to develop an AIDS hospice here at Mildmay. I'm very interested in the whole area of terminal care, and whilst I have only been involved in the care of two AIDS patients in Southend, I realise what a challenge there is in caring for people with this terrible disease.'

The present Matron had been 'hanging on' for the last two years until the right person came along. They had been interviewing for twelve months and had not been successful in appointing. Apparently there were more suitable applicants this time around, with the closing date in two days' time. As I left they said, 'We hope you will apply for the post.'

What was I to do? I had only been the District Nursing Manager in Southend for six months. My boss was not going to be very pleased. Did I really want to commute to London every day, especially on 'the misery line'? I had worked for the NHS most of my working life. Did I really want to give up that security to work for an independent Christian charity? What about my superannuation payments? Mildmay was not part of the NHS. What about sickness benefit? I would have to start from scratch again.

I had little time to consult with friends, but my colleagues just could not understand why I was applying for this job. To them it seemed a retrograde step and they strongly advised me to stay where I was. They knew I was a Christian and that my faith influenced my actions, but they still saw it as a mistake for me even to consider applying. I had doubts myself. 'Are you sure you really want me to do this Lord?' I asked. 'They won't want me as one of their Christian leaders.' The Mildmay I had known would not have selected a person separated from her husband as one of their top managers. I had been parted from my husband and children for two years and those two years had been the most painful of my life. During that time I found it very difficult to communicate with God, even at a time when I needed Him so much. For the last six months, however, I had been worshipping at a new church, reading the Bible and communicating with God again.

I was still hesitating about the job when I received a phone call from the Matron at Mildmay. 'I was just wondering whether you were going to apply, because we wanted you to know we would be prepared to give you another day in case you can't get your application in on time?' What a surprise! It seemed as though they were quite keen on me, but they still didn't know about my marital situation.

The Medical Director did, however. I had told her when I met her that I was separated from my husband and my children, but that it had never affected my work and I had not had a day's sick leave as a result. If anything, I had put all my efforts into my work so that I did not have to think about anything else. I told her that if I applied I would not raise this as an issue at interview as I thought it was unnecessary.

Decisions

Bearing all this in mind, and buoyed up by a feeling of closeness with God, I applied for the job and was invited for interview. All was going well when one of the panel looked at me and said, 'I see from your application form that you have four children, Ruth. I also have four children. Tell me about yours?'

I did a bit of quick thinking and realised that I had no choice but to tell them the situation. I had paused and you could have heard a pin drop as I started: 'You see, I'm not living with my family; my children are living with my husband, but it's a long story and I don't think we have the time and I'm not sure this is the place to tell you about it. I can tell you, however, that it has

not affected my work in a negative way. I have had no time off
from work.'

The reply soon came: 'We would like to give you the time if
you felt you could tell us about it.' The Medical Director,
knowing what I had said to her before, very kindly said, 'Only
if you want to.'

When I had finished telling my story, the man with four
children turned to me and said something amazing. He said,
'What a tremendous amount you will have to bring to this
place, to help those with pain and brokenness whom we will
care for in Mildmay.' Here was someone who was not condemn-
ing me, but who seemed to be saying the bad things that had
happened to me could be used for good. I began to feel that
I was of value, something I had not experienced for a long
time.

When the interview terminated, the panel were very positive
and told me they would be letting the successful candidate
know within twenty-four hours. There had been some very
good candidates for the post – I had spent time with them in
reception! On the way home I had a wonderful feeling of peace
and closeness to God. I was certain I had not got the job, but I
said to God, 'This whole episode has brought me so much
nearer to you. Please don't let me go again. Help me to be
obedient.'

That evening at 8.00 p.m. the phone rang. I answered it,
thinking it would be my daughter, but a voice said, 'Is that you
Ruth? This is Veronica Moss. We would very much like to offer
you the post of Matron.' I nearly deafened her with my joyous
response. How wonderful – they wanted me!

Being appointed to that post meant to me that I had been
chosen, I had been accepted as being the right person for that
work. Over the previous two years, I had learnt what rejection
and isolation meant, and the warmth and value of feeling
accepted made such a difference to me. I believe it changed my
whole life. Now I also know that for many of our patients with
AIDS, to be accepted changes their lives, and it is our privilege
to be part of that process.

Background to AIDS care at Mildmay

How had Mildmay first become interested in providing services for people with AIDS? Quite simply, Helen Taylor Thompson had been approached by Care Trust, a Christian organisation, with the suggestion that Mildmay might consider the possibility of being involved in the care of people with AIDS. Once interest had been stirred up, consultations were held with the District General Manager of Tower Hamlets Health Authority and a professor at the London Hospital, together with other doctors from the Royal London Hospital and other major centres in London such as St Stephen's and St Mary's Hospitals. (The London Hospital was the original name. When it became a Trust the name changed to the Royal London Hospital Trust. On its merger with St Bartholomew's Hospital in 1995 the name changed again to the Royal Hospitals Trust.)

Dr Moss had also discussed the project early on with the current staff and chronically sick patients at Mildmay. The response was positive. One profoundly disabled patient said to her, 'No one wanted us out there, did they? You care for us; why shouldn't you care for them?'

In January 1987, therefore, the decision was made to convert the ward previously known as Coventry into a hospice for people with AIDS. It was clear that it would not be a good idea to 'send people to coventry', so the ward was renamed Elizabeth Ward after Elizabeth Willcocks, the former Matron.

Mildmay employed an architect to draw up some provisional plans for converting the ward into the AIDS hospice unit. The Chairman of the Hospital, together with the Medical Director and the architect, were sponsored to visit San Francisco, where services for people with AIDS had already been developed and could be seen at first hand. Their purpose was to study the hospice, home nursing and counselling services and to consult with appropriate people about Mildmay's proposed provision. As a result of the visit, the original proposal written by Dr Moss was adjusted in the light of new information and she had further talks with staff and patients to keep them informed about the developments.

When I joined the team in April 1987, there were thirty staff in post. Mathieson Ward, on the first floor, could admit up to twenty-two patients, who were cared for in three bays of four and two single rooms, with eight beds for GP patients at the open end. Tankerville Ward, on the second floor, was empty but options were being considered for its use. As Matron I was responsible for overseeing the nursing care of the patients on Mathieson and for developing the care strategy for Elizabeth Ward.

How were we to go about setting up an AIDS hospice? It had been decided that we would have nine single room units, mostly with en suite facilities, with a counselling, pastoral and home care service, but that was as far as we had got. There were no hospices specialising in the care of people with AIDS in the UK, or indeed in Europe, and in fact at that time there were only three main acute hospitals with designated units. It seemed to me that the best way I could learn about the needs of people with AIDS and appropriate responses was by visiting San Francisco myself.

San Francisco

I believe very strongly that if God wants you to do a specific task, He will always equip you to do it. I knew from the nursing journals that Help the Hospices were offering scholarships to two British nurses to study issues concerning HIV and AIDS, so I duly prepared a project proposal and was invited for interview.

I was delighted to be awarded one of the scholarships and went to work for one month with the AIDS team of the Visiting Nurses Association in San Francisco. I spent a week of that month at the Coming Home Hospice, newly opened to care for people with AIDS. Previously I had only cared for two people with AIDS, and even then had not personally been providing hands-on care. But by now I knew quite a lot about AIDS and certainly knew how it was and was not transmitted. Nonetheless, I clearly remember the first time I went into the kitchen of the Coming Home Hospice to have a cup of coffee with the patients. I was told, 'Help yourself to a cup of coffee.' There were no clean cups. I looked at the cups lying in the sink and thought, 'Help, the patients have been using those.' I washed a cup and made myself some coffee, but I wasn't comfortable as I drank. Such is the power of inexperience and fear, despite the knowledge I had.

I made friends with many of the patients and I remember one of them in particular. He was a young man with many lesions of skin cancer (Kaposi's sarcoma) on his face. I was about to leave when he came across to me and gave me a hug and a kiss on my cheek. Although I knew his lesions were not infectious, I was frightened of his face touching mine. I think I washed the same area of my cheek ten times! How groundless those fears were, but talking with people in the same field, it seemed that most of us suffered from such irrational fears in those early days. It was something I needed to be aware of back at Mildmay.

During that month I visited so many people with AIDS. I saw people living alone, dying in practically derelict, box-like 'hotel' rooms. I saw patients being cared for by their partners, or by their mothers or friends. I saw wonderful care being given. One day when I was visiting a home, I spoke to the elderly lady who came to sit with me in the lounge while the nurse was treating the patient. 'Are you his mother?' I asked her.

'No,' she said, 'I am not. Sadly my son Peter died six months ago and Bill (this patient) was his partner. Bill loved Peter, you see, and cared for him so unselfishly – he gave up his job to help me look after him. Bill cared for him when he was pouring diarrhoea, had bed sores and was confused. Peter and Bill knew that they both had AIDS, and I made a promise to Peter that whenever Bill needed care, I would be there for him, and so here I am. You see his mother and father have disowned him, even though they know he is dying, so he is alone. He has no one but me.'

I went from house to house and saw fridges and cupboards

full of 'miracle cures', purchased by young men who had spent all their savings in an effort to stay alive. I was very affected by the youth of the patients. Some of them were desperately emaciated, their hair falling out, their eyes dull, looking so old. When I compared them with photographs of themselves as handsome, healthy young men, I realised anew what a terrible disease this was.

Jon's story

I learnt a great deal by spending one day with a patient at the Coming Home Hospice. Let me tell you how it went.

'You'd better watch out when you go into his room. He's very angry; he may or may not speak to you, but if he does he may probably swear at you. He probably won't let you do anything for him – he hasn't let us wash him for two weeks; the only thing we have done is change his diaper from time to time.' So spoke the care assistant at the hospice as she gave my assignment for the day, which was to help her care for Jon. Jon was twenty-eight years old, an ex-drug user who had AIDS. He was terminally ill, had refused to get out of bed for the last month and it was thought that he would probably die within the next few days.

Jon was not in contact with any friends or family and so he had no visitors. I was also told that his pressure areas were vulnerable and sores were developing as he was refusing to be turned. He was painfully thin, but refusing to eat. He had Kaposi's sarcoma and retinitis which was causing visual impairment, and he was *very* angry.

I walked up to his room, feeling a little apprehensive, and knocked on the door. Receiving no answer, I walked in. He looked at me and I introduced myself. 'Hello, Jon, I'm Ruth, I've come to look after you today. Can I sit with you a little while?' He continued to stare at me in stony silence while I sat down. At least he was not swearing. After a while he said to me, 'Get me a drink of milk.' I went downstairs and got him a glass of milk. As I was about to give it to him, he looked at me as though I was an absolute imbecile and said, 'Not a small glass you fool, I want a big one.' When I returned with his large glass of milk, he drank it all and gave the glass back to me. Then he just lay there, staring into space.

I noticed two things. He was fidgeting, obviously uncomfortable, and his left eye was puffy and infected. After a while he said to me, 'Change my diaper.' When I had everything ready, I pulled down the sheet and was upset to see the condition he was in. His penis was sore, there was diarrhoea dried all down his legs and groin, and as I turned him to remove the diaper I saw he had a pressure sore. His buttocks were bleeding and raw.

'Jon,' I said to him, 'I really can make you more comfortable if you'll let me. If I give you a good wash and put some cream on your back before I put on a clean diaper, you really will be more comfortable.' He glared at me and after what seemed an age he swore and said, 'Get on with it, then.'

I was so pleased to be able to clean him up and to treat his broken skin with a soothing cream. I washed his feet and cut his toenails, surprised all the time that he allowed me to do this. As I rolled him to put on his clean diaper I also rolled in a clean sheet. When I had completed the task, I thought, 'In for a penny, in for a pound,' and said to him, 'How about me making your top half more comfortable?'

Again he said, 'Get on with it.' I washed him and bathed his sore eye. As I put a fresh pyjama jacket on him, he said, 'I don't want that, I'm going out.'

'Going out?' I repeated.

'Yes, what's the matter with you, woman, are you deaf?'

'Do you feel strong enough to go out? You haven't been out of bed for four weeks!'

'I'm going out,' was all he would say.

I removed the equipment I was using and went to see the nurse in charge. She was very surprised when I told her what had happened to Jon, and that he said he wanted to go out, but she immediately said, 'Well, take him. I'll help you put him in the chair when you're ready.'

What happened next with Jon taught me a lesson I have never
forgotten, and this is why I have told the story in such detail. I
went up to him again and said, 'All right Jon, let me help you
get ready to go out.' He indicated where his clothes were and I
went to get his underwear out. Having selected a pair of boxer
shorts and a pair of socks, I put them on the bed. He screamed
at me, 'Not those! I will not have those!' When I had calmed
him down, I understood that he wanted the white boxer shorts
with the red lips on them. No others would do. He did not want
the grey socks, he wanted the white ones. He wanted the navy
joggers and the red sweatshirt with the hood.

Jon taught me how important it was for me to allow him to
make his own choices and not to impose my choices on him.
How could I be so thoughtless? This man now had so little
control over his environment and life, and here was I taking
away what little independence and control he could have. Back
at Mildmay, we would have to keep this vital principle constantly in mind.

When Jon was dressed, we transferred him to the chair and
Dave, one of the social workers, said he would like to come out
with us. Jon wanted the hood of his sweatshirt on to hide his
balding head, even though it was a very hot day. He insisted we
went to the supermarket, where he bought some drinking
chocolate and spent a long time deliberating over which ice
cream he would buy. In the end he couldn't make up his mind,
so he decided to go without. The supermarket was crowded and
we had quite a problem manoeuvring the wheelchair, so we
were pleased when Jon had paid the bill, which he insisted on
doing himself, and we got outside again. We had moved a few
steps along the road when he said, 'I want that ice cream.'

'Which one?' I asked. 'I'll go and get it for you.'

'You won't, I'll go and get it myself,' was the reply.

When we eventually emerged, Jon was holding tightly to his
carrier bag containing his chocolate drink and ice cream. As we
were walking back we passed a florist and a man ran up to us
to give Jon a single red rose. 'This is for you,' he said. Jon said
nothing, but his eyes filled with tears.

He died just two days later.

That special day I spent with Jon stands out so clearly in my memory, but I saw so much during my time in San Francisco, and learnt an enormous amount to take back to Mildmay.

In San Francisco I certainly saw the very best and worst of care, and I started to learn how to differentiate between the two. I now realised that the care of people with AIDS was very different to the care of other patients. I consulted in detail with patients, their carers and the planners of care provision. I observed, listened and read much which was to help us in the development of services at Mildmay. Whilst I was working with the nurses, the Medical Director of Mildmay attended a programme for doctors at San Francisco General Hospital which was being directed by Professor Volberding, a leader in the field of AIDS medicine. This also proved enormously beneficial.

Edinburgh

Our experiences in San Francisco mainly focused around the specific needs of gay men who had AIDS, but we knew that we would also be caring for people who had a history of intravenous drug use. During 1985 and 1986 it had become known that there were many HIV-infected drug users in Edinburgh. What better place to learn how to respond to their particular needs than on site, in Edinburgh? The Medical Director and I again obtained sponsorships to spend a week looking at the situation there. We visited drop-in centres, a ward at City General Hospital (the ward where most patients with AIDS were cared for) and other projects supporting drug users who were HIV positive or had AIDS.

I remember visiting a support group for drug users who were HIV positive and being profoundly affected by the age of the clients. The oldest was eighteen and the youngest fifteen years of age. The oldest was a beautiful, slim girl who had a lovely face with perfect skin and naturally blonde hair. She was clearly 'stoned' – her blue eyes were glazed and her gait was unsteady. When asked by the GP leading the group if she had been using drugs, she admitted she had just injected into her arm a solution made from temazepam tablets.

Two of the boys told the group that they had been shouting and swearing in their GP's surgery, where they had gone to collect their maintenance dose of methadone, and that they had been asked to leave. They were very indignant as they had been told they would be taken off that doctor's register. 'It's not fair,' they were saying, 'the people in the surgery were talking about us, saying why should we be given care and that people like us should be kept away from decent people. What were we supposed to do, sit there and take it?'

It was heartbreaking to see these youngsters, knowing that as well as being intravenous drug users, they were also HIV positive and that their lives would be cut short prematurely.

Planning operations at Mildmay

The visit to Edinburgh was very useful in helping us formulate our operational policies, because it became clear that we would have to think carefully through a number of issues if we were to care effectively for this client group, i.e. drug users. Among these difficult issues were pain control for patients addicted to heroin, the use and sale of illegal drugs on the unit, non-compliance, manipulation and antisocial behaviour. Principles learned in Edinburgh included: the importance of 'setting boundaries' or 'making contracts' with some drug users; and the need to avoid having more than one or two drug users on the same ward at any one time as the possibility of drug selling or passing on of drugs, or of conflict, increased with increasing numbers.

During the year we were busy recruiting the staff who would work on the hospice unit and by the end of the year we had prepared training programmes for all staff, including porters, domestic staff, receptionists, secretaries and clinical care staff. Included in the programmes were the following issues:

- the nature of terminal care and hospice care
- what is meant by improving the quality of life

- AIDS – the disease and its treatment
- how AIDS is transmitted – myths and facts
- the needs of people with AIDS and their families
- caring for people with AIDS and their families
- stigma and prejudice
- attitudes of the carers, and caring for the carers
- bereavement and loss

We had decided on a model of interdisciplinary care, centred on the principle of giving control back to patients, thereby enabling them to make informed decisions about their own care. This meant staff would have to ensure that they were knowledgable and up to date on development in a rapidly changing arena of care. We were aware that many people with AIDS knew far more about the disease and its treatment than those caring for them. Means of keeping staff up to date include regular in-house courses, opportunities of attending conferences, both national and international, work placements and visits to other centres and developing our own library and resource centre.

The interdisciplinary team at that time consisted of doctors, nurses, a counsellor, chaplain, occupational therapist, physio-therapist, housekeeper and supporting staff. A clinical nurse specialist was also appointed. The plan was to practise primary nursing, which meant that patients would get to know their own team of nurses and continuity of care could be established.

With a unit of only nine beds, it was obvious that only a small number of patients could benefit from our specialist care at any one time. We therefore realised it was very important for care to be linked to education, in order to broaden the benefits of our work. This education was to be given by those with first-hand experience in the field and was to be available to health care professionals and others. If we set up a series of 'external' conferences and seminars we could successfully target GPs, and hospice doctors and nurses, as well as ensuring sufficient education for our own staff. We planned to establish this education work by organising a major conference on AIDS care to coincide with the opening of the Elizabeth Unit, with the foremost speakers on AIDS in the UK invited to address us.

A Christmas break

A welcome break from all our frantic planning came at Christmas, a very special occasion that year. The small staff had many celebrations both as a team and with the patients. In addition to that, Mildmay continued as it had done for the previous two years to provide lunch and tea on Christmas Day in the Buxton Hall for up to a hundred local senior citizens who otherwise would be alone. The President, the Chairman, the management team, several of the staff and many volunteers gave up their Christmas Day to serve the old people. They were due to arrive at 11.00 a.m. for coffee and, whilst most of them were collected by car, those who could walk turned up at reception from 8.00 a.m. onwards! It was a day of hilarity and hard work, and it was truly worthwhile. Our guests all had coffee, mince pies, a three-course Christmas lunch with all the usual trimmings and a cup of tea with a piece of Christmas cake, while they watched the Queen's speech on a large screen. Entertainment was provided, and Father Christmas (from the local Rotary Club) brought them presents. The League of Friends of Mildmay funded the event and provided everyone with Christmas stockings and gifts of food, so they were well stocked in more ways than one when they returned home. It was a privilege to be able to show these elderly people that God cared about them too through His servants. This, I felt, was the real spirit of Mildmay, whoever was being cared for.

Dealing with hostility

Away from the joy of that special Christmas experience, however, it was not all plain sailing in the early stages of our AIDS unit. It had been a momentous decision for the Board of this small Christian hospital to take on the care of people with AIDS, and in the immediate future those connected with Mildmay sometimes felt they were crossing a minefield. On the one hand there were the Christians who were writing in and saying, 'Mildmay should never have got involved in this sort of thing. If you are caring for people with AIDS you are condoning their lifestyles.' On the other hand there were gay activists who were suspicious and hostile, asking what our hidden agenda was. Although there were only a few in both groups, they were extremely vocal and caused many problems. If they had had their way, we would never have established the service.

Staff were sometimes 'set up', and they would find people from both groups in audiences they had gone to address. Once the Medical Director was invited to appear on television at Mildmay to talk about the work, only to find that a campaigner who had never visited Mildmay to talk to us, but who was judging us before we had ever begun our work, had also been invited.

Our response to these situations was to remind people firmly that our remit was to care for people with AIDS, and that the arena of terminal care was not the place for debate about lifestyle unless it was causing a problem for the patient and he or she wished to discuss it with someone. We asked people who were hostile to us to allow us to get on with the work we believed God wanted us to do. As 'the proof of the pudding would be in the eating', if they found cause for complaint when our services were provided, we would certainly address the matter then. Usually, when people came to see us, we could allay their fears.

In view of the fear and prejudice we were experiencing elsewhere, one encouragement we had was from Mildmay's current young disabled patients. It had been necessary to consult them because we were going to introduce the care of people with AIDS alongside another client group. Whilst this might normally be an act of courtesy, there was quite a different motivation because the new group were people with AIDS. We felt vastly cheered by their warm and positive response.

Support and opposition notwithstanding, we faced a tough challenge at Mildmay. I mentioned that AIDS is different,

unique, and it is in many ways. The client group is a young one
– babies, small children, and teenagers to young adults. Many
live alone and are lonely and isolated. They live secret lives for
fear of persecution. The expectation of compassion from people
who know you have a terminal illness is not there for those
with AIDS. They know they will die prematurely, but they long
to live and will give everything they have in the hope of staying
alive. Many of them have nursed partners and friends who have
died of AIDS, and life seems to focus on one loss after another.
Independence and control over their lives seems to be disappearing, and many of them have barely discovered what independence is.

The decision in January 1987 for Mildmay to be involved in
the care of people with AIDS was a turning point for this
insignificant, Christian charitable hospital. Despite the opposition, the project went ahead under God's guidance and
provision. He called together people who wanted to work with
people with AIDS, and who had all the right skills to bring to
the team. Many were brought from good, secure positions into
apparent insecurity, but they came, ready to serve God and
those people crying out for care.

2

A TIME OF CONFLICT AND NEW UNDERSTANDING 1987–8

Facing up to opposition

'It just missed her head, Matron. She could have been killed,' said the Sister. I was standing in the lounge on Mathieson Ward with the Ward Sister and one of our young patients. Aged twenty-six, she had been paralysed from the neck downwards following surgery for a tumour. There was very little she could do for herself, but she was learning to live with her disability and was finding new areas where she could be independent.

She was sitting in her wheelchair now, crying and trembling with fear. A brick had just been thrown through the window and had missed her by inches. Can you imagine what it must be like to have such an experience, when you are unable in any way to remove yourself from danger? Thankfully neither she nor any other patient in the room was physically injured, but they were all emotionally battered.

This was not the first time a brick had been thrown through our windows recently. Since it had become known through the local newspaper that we were going to care for people with AIDS, we had received abuse in various ways. Youngsters from nearby tower blocks had been shouting, 'AIDS! AIDS!' followed by various derogatory comments. Bricks and stones were hurled through the windows and abuse was shouted at people seen in the grounds of the hospital. All this was before we had even started caring for patients with AIDS. In a way I was grateful it was happening now, because I hoped that people might work through it before we actually had patients on site.

We asked the porters to keep an eye on the grounds and try

to talk to the people who were being abusive, inviting them in to meet us so that we could discuss any problems they had. One of the porters was able to do just that. Paul was a young man who had taught in the Sunday School of the local church. He confronted a group of teenagers who had stones in their hands and were clearly about to throw them at the windows. Amongst the group were some youngsters who had been in his Sunday School class a few years before. Paul asked them if they realised what they were doing by throwing stones and said he would like to show them something. They agreed to go with him.

Having obtained the permission of the Ward Sister and the patients, Paul took this small group of boys up to Mathieson Ward, where he introduced them to some of the patients in the lounge: young people in wheelchairs, some sitting in specially adapted armchairs, a boy of twenty-two, paralysed following a road accident, and another in his twenties with advanced multiple sclerosis. All were unable to move without help or to protect themselves from danger. When the boys had been shown round, Paul took them down to his room off the reception area. He didn't need to say very much to them, only, 'Can you imagine how you would feel if you were one of those people and bricks and stones came suddenly flying through the windows?' Although abuse continued to be shouted, from the roofs of the tower blocks, we had no more episodes of broken windows or abuse being shouted in the grounds themselves.

The Chairman of Mildmay was by now receiving some letters that were causing her a great deal of distress. The letters were from Mildmay supporters who had real problems with Mildmay becoming involved in caring for people with AIDS. One gentleman wrote continuously over a period of weeks, quoting the Bible to her and writing about AIDS as the judgment of God. Every letter was answered, with an explanation that we were doing only what we believed God wanted us to do, and we believed it was a privilege to be able to care for people with AIDS. In every situation we would ask, 'What would Jesus have done?' and we know that Jesus healed the sick, cared for those in need and demonstrated love, acceptance and compassion. He also said to us, 'Do not judge, and you will not be judged' (Luke 6:37). Eventually this particular man withdrew his support for Mildmay's work. What sadness this attitude caused. Some others joined him, but I am glad to say it was limited to a very few of our many supporters.

By the end of the year we had appointed the nurses who were going to work on Elizabeth Ward, although we were still not open to patients. One day one of them came up to me looking very upset. She had her coat on and was just coming into the building. 'I've just been to the dentist,' she said, 'and when I gave my new address of Mildmay Nurses' Home, he refused to see me. When I asked him why he wouldn't see me, he said, "I'm not seeing anyone from Mildmay".'

Another significant situation occurred around that time, when two of the nurses on Mathieson Ward took Bobby (one of our patients) round to the local barber for his monthly haircut. As the nurses wheeled him in, the barber said, 'I'm sorry I can't do it any more.' When the nurses asked him why, he replied, 'I know 'e ain't got AIDS, but if my customers know that I've got anybody in 'ere from that Mildmay, I'll lose my business. Sorry girl, I can't afford to do that.'

Stories were also coming back to me about taxi drivers who were refusing to pick anyone up from Mildmay, and they had even refused a fare when somebody had asked to be taken to Mildmay. There was so much prejudice about.

Sheila and Bill

Sheila was a dear friend of mine, a warm, loving Christian lady who had had a sad life. Her husband had left her to bring up her son, Bill, on her own. Bill had gone to Sunday School as a child and as an adult believed in God and occasionally went to church with his mother. When Bill was twenty years old, he told her that he was gay. He said he had been reluctant to tell her because he wasn't sure how she would react, and as she was a Christian, he felt her attitude would be one of disapproval.

It did take her some time to come to terms with the information. She wanted to be sure that he wasn't being persuaded or forced by anyone else into a way of life that she thought would involve so much loss. Eventually she accepted what he said because, looking back, she realised he had been rather effeminate, not a good mixer, and over the last year or two he had behaved as though something was wrong, although he would just say, 'I'm OK, Mum, don't keep on so.'

Sheila was a very committed Christian and a woman who talked to God about everything. She prayed every day for Bill, asking God to protect him as he tried to cope with the many problems he had.

When Bill brought home his first partner, Sheila had a lot of adjusting to do. 'It's one thing to have a son who says he's homosexual, that in itself was relatively easy to accept, because I really believed for Bill he had no choice, he didn't want to be homosexual, and he didn't choose to be homosexual . . .' She realised, however, that if she did not accept someone who was important to Bill, she would probably lose Bill as well, and so she became quite a support and help to them both.

When that relationship broke up, Bill was distraught. He was a loner and found it very difficult to make friends. He lived in a flat not far from his mother and during the next few months they became quite close. He then told her that he and his former partner had been very upset, because they had been to a couple of churches together and had been made to feel very unwelcome. 'People stared at us, Mum, and once, when we were holding hands, there was a lot of whispering and black looks over in our direction. You know I believe in God, Mum, and I have this feeling, I want to go to church, but I can't.'

Sheila could understand that the one thing Bill couldn't handle was rejection, so she suggested to him that perhaps he would allow her to have a chat with her vicar about the situation and then take it from there. Bill agreed and Sheila saw her vicar, who said that Bill would be very welcome at the church. The first time he went with her, they sat together in a pew. The vicar greeted Bill by name at the end of the service, and Bill enjoyed the experience and said to his mother that he would like to go again.

The next time they went there was a service of Holy Communion. Bill felt he would like to take Communion, so he and his mother took their place in the queue of communicants moving to the front of the church. When they both knelt in front of the rail, the vicar gave the bread to Sheila, but when he reached Bill he said, 'Are you a practising homosexual?' The vicar had a portable microphone clipped to the front of his surplice and, although he spoke quietly, Bill was not the only one who heard the question. Sheila quietly took Bill's hand and together they walked out of the church. Bill has never been to church since, but Sheila did return. She explained to me that she felt like never returning, but she could not let that sort of thing happen to anyone else if there was anything she could do to prevent it. 'My pain, which includes the shame I feel at the way that vicar treated my son, is nothing compared to the pain that Bill feels,' she said.

Confronting our own prejudices

During these early stages, we at Mildmay encountered many new situations and problems and had to address issues we had never considered before. The staff as individuals had to look hard at their own attitudes and prejudices before dealing with other people's. It was necessary to come to terms with the fact that the arena of care for people with AIDS was complicated by stigma, prejudice, ignorance and fear, often resulting in conflict and hostility, as the above stories show.

When I came to Mildmay I had certainly never really thought about some issues with which I was confronted. Other staff were in a similar position. I had never worked with drug users and whilst I had a few friends and colleagues who I knew were homosexual, I had never given the issue much thought. I asked God to guide me and direct my thinking as I considered my own attitudes and prejudices. I asked for understanding and compassion and the ability to learn from my environment and the people I met. In the induction programme for new staff we made sure there were workshops helping people to look at their own attitudes and prejudices.

As a manager I realised that all staff would need proper support to work effectively in this highly stressful arena. We needed a structure and staffing establishment that would enable staff to have time to care. As a step towards this, we decided to appoint a part-time staff counsellor, who would be there to facilitate support groups and work with individuals as necessary. However, there was a balance to be struck: it was going to be no use providing emotional support if what was needed was another pair of hands. One way to ensure sufficient pairs of helping hands was to make use of volunteers. During our visit to San Francisco I had noticed just how much volunteers were used to assist in the provision of care. In London the Terence Higgins Trust was already well known for its Buddying service, which was provided by volunteers to people with AIDS. During our months of preparation we had received many offers of voluntary help and we were concerned that, if we did use volunteers, we would provide them with adequate training and support, along with the paid staff. Shirley Lunn, our counsellor, was responsible for developing the volunteer service. She advertised in the local papers, church notice boards and in our own literature, and received 263 applications. From these we selected our first thirty volunteers, and a training programme was designed for them. Ten training sessions were to be offered per course and at the end of that time the volunteers could work on the AIDS unit, or elsewhere in the hospital.

The rôle and example of Mildmay

Some people seem to think that Mildmay is a kind of church and have condemned it for not making statements and providing biblically based teaching about certain issues. We are not a church and we believe God's work at Mildmay is primarily about providing holistic (whole person) care to people with AIDS and their families. This involves responding to spiritual and emotional needs as well as social ones, but sensitivity must be exercised in these areas – hence our rigorous training and education plans. The spiritual needs of a patient are as he or she perceives them and the response to those needs must be at the initiation of and acceptable to the individual patient.

The whole moral issue surrounding homosexuality and the Church's attitude to it is definitely not Mildmay's debate, but it becomes a problem for us when individuals we care for are affected by discrimination and prejudice. If we cannot walk with people, how can we ever help them? Unconditional acceptance is about caring for someone, now, as they are, and not about saying, 'I will accept you and care for you only if you conform to my standards and code of behaviour.' As professional medical staff, we cannot impose our standards or our beliefs on the people for whom we care. We do not do this for any other group of patients, so why should we do it for people with AIDS?

I feel that the way we have constantly been challenged about lifestyle issues and faced with prejudice has, at times, hindered us from getting on with the work of caring that I believe God has given us to do at Mildmay. I know from my own experience that it was easier working with patients with cancer or other diseases. It would never have entered anyone's head, when faced with someone dying of lung cancer, to say to them, 'Well of course, you have brought this on yourself.' Or to say to an obese person who has had a heart attack, 'Well of course, it's your own fault really, you have always eaten too much.' In this country we generally care for dying people with compassion and sensitivity. Why, then, does it have to be so different for people with AIDS?

We felt sure that education was the best way to combat ignorance and prejudice, and the following example showed this to be correct. In a discussion with staff I learned that many of their families and friends were anxious about them working at Mildmay with people with AIDS. We decided to hold an Open Evening to which we invited them all. The nursing team produced some skits which showed a variety of situations where care was needed as well as situations where there was no risk of transmission of the virus. During the following question time it became evident that the evening had been very necessary and was dealing with genuine anxieties and fear.

It made us keenly aware of just how afraid many people were of getting AIDS through social contact. Although reason and knowledge informed them of the modes of transmission, when confronted with the situation unreasonable fears overwhelmed them. My own experience in San Francisco supports this theory. Was it because the only exposure most people in this country had to AIDS was to see the terrible pictures of Rock Hudson and others looking so ill and obviously suffering? And for those who were personally caring for someone, those fears would be compounded without adequate education and support. That is where Mildmay had such an important rôle to play. Even some nurses and doctors were refusing to go near or care for people with AIDS, while some just felt inadequate when faced with the prospect. We believed that education could change that, and Mildmay would be in a prime position to provide education for those who needed it.

In terms of the patients themselves, we very much wanted to encourage a positive approach. We learned in America, and it was reinforced back home, just how important it was to encourage people to live with AIDS rather than sitting around waiting to die once they had been given the diagnosis. In San Francisco I had seen a board with bright yellow stars on it in the office of a social worker at the Coming Home Hospice. In the middle of each star was a name. I asked her to tell me what it was for, and she said that each star represented a person who had died with them. We decided that at Mildmay we would not place such emphasis on remembering death, but rather on remembering life. We therefore decided that we would have a book of remembrance and into that book would go the name of everyone who had *lived with* us.

To sum up just briefly, then: we saw our rôle at Mildmay as providing (a) care without prejudice for the whole person, (b) education as necessary for as broad a public as possible, and (c) fostering a positive approach to life, illness and death.

Understanding the hostility

If we were to take on an educational rôle, then we needed to start by understanding the opposition from those closest to us. The initial hostile response from members of the local community did not really surprise us. Perhaps the surprise was that so few people responded in a negative way. We had thought that it might be necessary to hold public meetings to inform and reassure members of the local community about our proposals, but in the event it proved unnecessary. We had expected that there would be a great deal of resistance locally to Mildmay caring for people with AIDS, but it certainly did not result in any media involvement or organised activity. Only groups of teenagers and just a few individuals made their feelings known, so we decided that to have public meetings might invoke more problems and hostilities. It was better to deal with cases individually.

So what was behind the responses of these few? I believe it was fear that was at the root of the problem. The hairdresser and the taxi drivers mentioned earlier were certainly fearful of contact with people with the virus. (I had even heard of people fumigating vehicles known to have carried people with AIDS.) I think that fear was also fed by ignorance of the facts. At that time, given the general level of education about the disease, the hairdresser was probably absolutely correct in saying that if his clients knew that people with AIDS were using the salon they would have removed their custom. In the case of the dentist, of course, his practice should have been of such a standard that he would be safe whoever he was treating. How could he know if *any* of his patients had HIV or other blood-borne infections? Surely the only safe way to practise would be to assume that everybody had the possibility of being infected, and then where was the need for prejudice towards individuals? With the young boys throwing bricks and stones, I would suggest that for many, their attitudes would have been 'inherited' from family members.

There was clearly a very real need for education about the

HIV disease and its transmission for members of the general public and particularly all those who were going to be involved in any way with Mildmay's new activities. The plans for the Education Department were progressing well and we were now considering how we might effectively communicate the essential facts about AIDS to those who needed to know – not only for the benefit of Mildmay and our patients, but for the wider good as well. Even before more formal plans were in place, we took care to invite those concerned to Mildmay, give them a cup of coffee, and encourage them to ask questions about our work. That way we could answer face to face any misapprehensions, and it proved a successful way to set the record straight.

Breaking down the barriers

Mildmay's staff were also being invited to address many groups about their proposed developments, and although these meetings could often be quite confrontational, the Lord enabled us to handle each situation, allay fears and enthuse people about our plans and vision. Rev. Peter Clarke had joined us as chaplain and was very supportive during this time.

I remember being invited to the local Buddy group. We met in someone's house and there were about twenty men there. One of them appeared to be extremely hostile to me and had a list of a dozen questions, to which he said they all wanted straight answers. I answered the questions, told them what we were proposing to do and how we were proposing to do it, and invited their comments. I also explained to them that Mildmay was going to provide care of a professional standard. Fully qualified doctors and nurses with a duty to care without discrimination would be looking after people with AIDS. They would all have chosen to do the job, and therefore I believed they would do it well. Patients and their wishes would be respected and we were already in consultation with people with AIDS to ensure that our services would truly be what they needed.

By the end of that evening I and Mildmay had many new

friends. Some are still my friends today, and they have helped us over the years with advice, fundraising ventures and voluntary assistance. They had been very worried that Mildmay might be getting involved with AIDS work, not primarily to care for people, but to corner gay men in order to preach at them.

In one of the gay newspapers (*Capital Gay*) we were described as the 'bad Samaritans', and the paper questioned whether gay men dying of AIDS would be safe in our hands. I was so upset by this article that I responded to it. I felt sure that the article would increase fear in people who were already apprehensive about coming to us, and anyway I felt that the comments were unfair and untrue. Part of my reply is quoted below:

I am glad the word 'safe' was used because it is a word that so aptly describes the environment we must create at Mildmay. Creating a safe environment is an integral part of total patient care. In order to do this one must consider what might prove to be barriers. Patients may come to us fearful and defensive, looking for signs of condemnation and rejection and these feelings could greatly inhibit their quality of life. The carer can break down or reinforce these barriers by his/her attitude. I think it is so important that we are not, and are not seen to be, judgmental. Whatever our personal feelings are, in the context of care as professionals, we have no right to even comment on a patient's lifestyle unless we are specifically invited to do so by the patient.

At Mildmay we will be dealing with people as individuals and plan their total care accordingly. It would, therefore, be very damaging to the welfare of a patient to indicate in any way that he/she is seen as just one of a group or category. In the article it was stated that 'I am sure that patients will get the best nursing care but the philosophy behind it is disturbing'. I also believe that patients will get the very highest standard of nursing care at Mildmay. Care for the whole person with physical, emotional, social and spiritual needs being catered for by a multi-disciplinary team of specialists. These carers are being specially selected from the many people who have expressed a real desire to work in this field of care. They are people who share my views on the necessity to care for people with unconditional love, accepting people as they are and learning about and understanding the needs and attitudes of patients from all backgrounds. They will be highly trained personnel.

What is it about our philosophy that is so disturbing? Perhaps I should comment on how we see our Christianity in practice at Mildmay. We believe that by giving the very highest standards of care to our patients, by creating a safe, secure environment for them and by loving them and providing for their needs as individuals we will demonstrate the love of God in a way that will speak louder than any words. If they wish to discuss spiritual or personal matters with us we will be happy to share with them, but generalising over how we would deal with individual situations is of little value and lacking in reality.

One thing we will do at Mildmay is to pray. Pray that our provision will be effective, that our patients will feel loved and cared for and know peace and serenity as they live in our hospice unit. For our accent at Mildmay is on living life to its full potential.

As time went on we began to understand so much more of the issues that were of concern for people with AIDS and the way that, even as care providers, we were going to be affected. I remember one of the greatest influences on me was meeting and talking to people who were HIV positive and had AIDS. I realised then that first impressions could be so very misleading. Attitudes changed after getting to know people properly.

I think the same applied to people who had problems with Mildmay: when they could talk and meet with us, situations were resolved. Certainly, as the year went on, many of our greatest critics became our closest friends. From conflict we moved to understanding, although at this stage, with the unit not yet open, we were still saying 'the proof of the pudding would be in the eating'.

Along with the moves to counter hostility and to clarify Mildmay's rôle, work of a more concrete nature had also, of course, been taking place. The work of refurbishment and commissioning was completed by the end of the year and the unit looked very attractive. We had achieved our objective to make it home-like and welcoming. Unfortunately the costs had increased enormously. The building had been built almost one hundred years earlier and every time the builders took something apart, they found it needed replacing or repairing. The original budget had been for £260,000, but it ended up costing over £600,000. Miraculously, voluntary donations covered the enormous deficit.

3

A TIME OF NEW BEGINNINGS
1988

Welcoming visitors

By the end of 1987 Elizabeth Unit was complete. All the necessary staff had been recruited and furnishings and fittings had been supplied. We decided to have a two-week period in January when visitors could come to Mildmay to see the unit. Once we had started admitting patients we would not be able to entertain visitors so freely. Some had even given as their reason for requesting a visit: 'I want to see someone with AIDS.' Others, more genuine, were developing services elsewhere, and we had soon realised that being involved in a pioneering venture would mean that people would want to see and learn from us. We felt we had a responsibility to share our experience with them, as others had shared their own knowledge with us.

During those two weeks in January we invited different groups of people to visit every day to have coffee or lunch with us. These included officials from the Department of Health, health care professionals from all disciplines, planners of services, supporters, staff family members and friends. One day was devoted to the media, and representatives of the major television companies and national and local newspapers attended. A great deal of interest was shown during this time and we received coverage on both BBC and ITV news programmes as well as many national and local newspapers and Christian journals.

We were very proud to show people the beautiful new unit with its homely, comfortable lounge and the latest in medical and nursing equipment. God had been so good in providing for our needs, both financial and in terms of manpower.

The first steps

On 28th February 1988 the first four beds on Elizabeth Ward were opened to patients and our first patient arrived that day. As he was the only patient he received a great deal of care and attention, so much so that he felt overwhelmed and decided to go home again the next day, assuring us that he had made a rapid recovery! He was readmitted again a few weeks later, however, and following a number of other respite admissions he was finally admitted for terminal care and died with us, about a year later. By this time he had become our friend and he said he felt at home, as though he was with family.

The first Annual Conference took place a few days after the opening of the unit and was held in the Mission Hall (renamed The Buxton Hall after a former Medical Superintendent, Dr Kenneth Buxton). In order to conform to fire regulations, we could only seat 250 people in there. The conference had been advertised in relevant journals and the response was enormous. We quickly filled our 250 places and had to turn dozens of people away. We did, however, make a profit of £13,500 on that Conference, as all the catering was provided from voluntary donations and overseen by Mrs Helen Taylor Thompson, the Chairman of our Board at the time, and a band of volunteers. Staff from all departments who could be spared took part in one way or another, from receiving participants and doing cloakroom and parking duties to serving coffee and giving out information packs. On the day before the conference the ground floor was a hive of activity. The porters were polishing floors and moving chairs. The Maintenance Manager, doubling as audio visual manager, was to be found carrying equipment, wires trailing everywhere! In the Buxton Hall people were practising their presentations, cutlery and crockery was being unpacked, and chairs were being put into place amidst peals of laughter and 'One, two, three, testing' coming over the loudspeakers. There was a real air of excitement at this, our first conference. On the day, everyone was wearing their smartest clothes and their badges and were proud to be part of Mildmay. There was a real team spirit about the place.

From that time onwards Mildmay had a reputation for providing wonderful food at conferences. This was partly due to the 'Mildmay cheesecake', made by Mrs Taylor Thompson herself, and the fact that she had made a special deal with a fisherman friend in Scotland who provided us with fresh salmon at £1.50 per pound! She was an absolute expert at getting something for nothing, and never had any reluctance to beg for things for Mildmay. At that time we had no idea just how much funding she personally, under God's direction, would be instrumental in raising.

During the following year I organised several more conferences which were very successful due to the excellent teamwork of the Mildmay staff. There were conferences for nurses, doctors, counsellors, church leaders and our own staff. This also proved to be a good way of generating income which could be invested in the development of the wider educational work.

One morning we received a telephone call from the office of the then Social Democratic Party leader, Dr David Owen, asking if he could visit Mildmay. The visit was arranged and I was very pleased to be able to show him around our two wards, introducing him to staff and those patients wishing to meet him. When we were in my office after the visit, he said to me with a grin, 'Oh, by the way, I wanted to let you know that I quoted you in my recent book, *Our NHS*!' He had quoted the following at the beginning of a chapter entitled 'Public Health': 'If you have disfiguring lesions on your face, you're ulcerated from your mouth to your anus and you're producing ten litres of diarrhoea a day – to encourage you to be brave and carry on living with dignity is going to take considerable skill, in my opinion.'

The opening ceremony

Within three months of opening four beds, our occupancy had increased and it was necessary to open the remaining five. We were now ready for the official ceremony to reopen Mildmay itself, and to open Elizabeth Ward.

Princess Alexandra had opened the extension to Mildmay in 1965 when it was still a District General Hospital, and so it was decided that she should be the one we would invite to reopen the new Mildmay. She graciously accepted, and so, on 19th May 1988, 250 invited guests gathered in the Buxton Hall where Bishop Maurice Wood conducted a dedication service. We then proceeded to Tankerville Ward, where the Princess unveiled a plaque and cut a special celebration cake. She met staff and volunteers, including members of Frontliners, a self-help group for people with AIDS who had a base on the Mildmay site. She talked with Peter Tillson, a person with AIDS, who was advisor to the Board on matters relating to the care of people with AIDS. He has continued to be a great friend to the hospital and always offered us good advice and counsel.

Princess Alexandra visited both Mathieson and Elizabeth Wards, talking to many patients and their families and friends. It was a very special day for patients and staff alike, and Mildmay was a happy place to be in, full of good humour, laughter and a real sense of celebration. I remember the secretaries and Kathy, the receptionist, having a 'knees-up' on Tankerville Ward after the Princess and guests had left. We had a wonderful feast, to which everyone on site was invited – no wonder that people coming to work at Mildmay tended to complain of putting on weight!

Media interest

The media interest in the opening of Elizabeth Ward, the overwhelming response to invitations to our open weeks and the way that the first Annual Conference was over-subscribed indicated to us that the general public were interested in, and wanted to know more about, the care of people with AIDS. Undoubtedly some of this interest was generated because Mildmay was Europe's first residential hospice for people with AIDS (the residential services at London Lighthouse opened six months later). Certainly the television advertising, information posted through letterboxes and media pictures of well-known figures with this killer disease had enhanced people's curiosity. After television coverage of Mildmay itself we were inundated afresh with requests for information and the chance to visit.

The response to the Annual Conference, which was primarily directed at health care professionals, was an indication of just how little people knew about AIDS and how keen they were to find out more. As the work of Mildmay developed and its reputation grew, so it attracted more and more visitors. Health care professionals came from all over the UK and abroad to learn about the care of people with AIDS.

In order to cope with the large numbers we held open afternoons where groups of people could see slides, meet members of the interdisciplinary team and discuss issues of particular interest over cups of tea. Initially we had one open afternoon a month, but when the numbers reached fifty on one day, we conducted the open afternoons weekly. Other people came to see me and other individual team members for personal discussion, which was very time consuming. As a result we commenced our work placement programmes, which enabled health care professionals to learn first hand. They were limited to monthly placements of one or two people and approval was always obtained before they were allowed to visit individual patients.

It was difficult at that time to make people understand the importance of our patients' need for privacy. We had a duty to protect them from being stared at, or having their privacy invaded by individuals or groups. They were not to be made to feel as though they were in a zoo. The stigma and prejudice experienced by our patients necessitated our taking extra care to ensure that confidentiality was not breached and that they would not be seen by anyone if they did not wish it. Our aim was that those we were caring for would live with us, not be stuck in their own rooms behind closed doors because they were frightened of who would see them in the lounge or dining area. In order to achieve that aim, visitors to the unit once it was opened, apart from patients' own visitors, were not encouraged. It was a pleasure, on going into the lounge, to see groups of patients relaxed and laughing together. Living, not sitting around waiting to die. One story might illustrate the sort of beneficial atmosphere and careful support we were hoping to achieve.

Julie

She was one of the first patients admitted to Elizabeth Ward for terminal care. Julie was in the day room of a designated AIDS ward in a central London hospital when I first saw her. She was asked by her doctor to return to her room so that we could talk to her about her referral to Mildmay. As she stubbed out her cigarette she glared at us both and said nothing. I cannot describe my feelings as I watched this young girl of twenty-five attempting to walk across the room. She was stooped, wasted and so weak that she could hardly walk. When the doctor and I tried to help her, she swore at us as she pushed us away and proceeded to move to her room, holding on to anything she could find on the way and resting from time to time.

When we got to her bed, it seemed to take ages for her to climb on to it, but her nonverbal communication made it very clear that she was determined to do it on her own. She was obviously very, very angry and suspicious of everyone. Once there, she appeared to listen as the doctor told her about Mildmay, occasionally looking up to glare at me, then looking away again. It seemed to me that those glares were full of hatred. 'What do I want to go there for? What can they do for me? Who do they think they are? Who does she think she is?' she said, looking at me. Then she said, 'Will I have my own room?'

'Yes, you will, and you will have your own toilet and handwash basin adjacent to it.'

'What about the grub?' she said with a snarl. 'I like what I like and not what I don't like – understand?'

I explained to her that she would be able to choose her own food from the menu and if there was something special that was not on the menu she would be able to order it in advance.

'What about this religion thing? I don't want any of it, understand. Are they funny people, are they friendly? And what about my fags? When I want a fag, I want a fag. Will I get my methadone?' She looked straight at me. 'What makes you think you can do anything for me?'

I told her we would like her to come to Mildmay so that she could benefit from the facilities there. We would offer her physiotherapy and aim to control the symptoms that were distressing her in order to make her more comfortable.

'I ain't bleedin' going there,' she retorted.

As she sat there, her large blue eyes staring angrily at me from such a small thin face, she reminded me of a waif, a stray, so vulnerable, so insecure. I realised that if she did come she would pose a real challenge to all of us, but also that there was something in her reaching out for love and acceptance.

During the year prior to Julie's assessment she had been in and out of hospital suffering from weakness, malaise and inability to cope with her numerous social and emotional problems. After several months she was tested, with her permission, and found to be HIV positive. Two months before, she had had pneumocystis carinii pneumonia, an AIDS defining illness, and her general condition had begun to deteriorate. She developed recurrent episodes of encephalitis, thought to be due to HIV infection.

A few days after my assessment visit Julie was admitted to Mildmay. On admission she was found to be quiet, withdrawn and passive. She was very thin; her hair was sparse and falling out and had recently been infested with head lice, her skin was dry and coarse and she admitted she was occasionally incontinent of urine. She said she had last used heroin nine months before and was now taking methadone twice a day.

'Have I got AIDS? I didn't know I had AIDS.' She then

quickly changed the subject. It was difficult to know then whether she was using denial as a way of coping or whether she had short-term memory loss.

When asked about her family and friends, she said, 'Mind your own bleedin' business, I don't want to know them, they don't want to know me, especially now as I'm ill.' Julie was the second of five children. She had three brothers and one sister. All her brothers attended schools for educationally subnormal children. Julie was by far the most intelligent member of the whole family and had found that position difficult, resulting in lack of effort at school and failure to achieve satisfactory results. Soon after her sister was born, her mother had a nervous breakdown and during the two years that followed, when Julie was about nine years old, her mother took five overdoses and slashed her wrists. When Julie was eleven, she was brought before the Juvenile Court for non-attendance at school. She had been staying at home to protect her younger sister from her father.

At twelve years old Julie, encouraged by her parents, dyed her hair, painted her finger and toenails, wore heavy make-up and started smoking cigarettes. She once said she would rather have been a boy because 'they have more choices'. She seldom wore dresses, mostly jeans and dungarees. By the time she was thirteen she had run away from home four times and belonged to a group of 'greasers'. She admitted at that age to have had sexual intercourse with over a dozen men, some of whom she refused to name. There were strong suspicions that members of her family were involved, probably why she felt she needed to protect her sister. She had her first termination of pregnancy and was given the Pill when she was thirteen years old. It was recorded that Julie had often been involved in fights and 'kicked in'. She spent most of the remainder of her early teenage years in children's homes.

When she was sixteen Julie ran away to London and quickly became a heroin addict. She funded this by prostitution and theft. She had one particular boyfriend, on and off, over the following years; he was also a drug user. A son was born to her when she was seventeen years old and was immediately adopted. She also became involved in what was to her a very meaningful same-sex relationship. She lived in squats and stated that her friends disappeared when she first became ill.

In Mildmay Julie was continually asking for diamorphine (heroin), and when she could not get that she asked for an increase in her doses of methadone. She complained of not feeling well and attributed everything to not having enough methadone. As she settled in, however, her need for methadone reduced and after one month she decided she would try to wean herself off it.

As her condition improved so did her appetite so that she was always wanting to eat. She became very demanding and began to use the buzzer to summon people at least once every hour. She became very manipulative and demanding and played staff off against each other. She often appeared to be frightened. We had to establish with her boundaries of acceptable behaviour, and once this was done I think she felt more secure.

She enjoyed lying in bed, eating toffees and drinking coke, smoking, watching the TV and reading comics and one day when I was on the ward I was told she had severe abdominal pain. I went to see her as I always did now, because we had established quite a close relationship. As I walked in she looked up, her mouth full of toffee and the usual opened can of coke on her locker.

'I hear you have stomach ache, Julie?'

'Yeah, it ain't 'alf bad, I dunno what to do.'

I looked at her and grinned. 'How about not stuffing yourself so full of sweets and coke, eh?'

She laughed. 'Shut up, you, you know don't yer?'

'Yes,' I said, 'I've got a couple at home your age!' She had a wonderful sense of humour.

Occasionally she would have problems with constipation or diarrhoea and she became so embarrassed. She coped with this loss of dignity in perhaps the only way she knew how, by becoming angry and abusive.

From her initial suspicion, however, Julie gradually learned to trust staff. She became popular and many of the staff who were not working on the ward would visit her and take her small presents – toffees and coke!

She seemed to prefer the company of women and older staff, perhaps because they represented the mother figure she never had. When asked how she was, she would often say, 'I'm bleedin' bored!' but she would seldom leave her room or get involved in other activities. She was frightened of being alone, or being rejected. I remember one day when I went into her room, she said to me, 'You ain't got a bleedin' chair, 'ave you?' I went and got one and we had a chat. This was her way of saying, 'Will you come and talk to me, will you sit down with me?' The way she handled it lessened her risk of being rejected by me saying, 'I'm sorry I haven't got time,' or something similiar.

Julie rarely had visitors except for one girl friend. Julie was very unpredictable where this girl was concerned, but although the friend visited her regularly Julie would often chuck her out or tell her not to come again. She would occasionally talk of the boyfriend she had but she refused to have him contacted. She commented once or twice that she wondered if she had infected him. He did find out where she was and rang to ask if he could visit her, but Julie adamantly refused, although he had travelled many miles in the hope that she would change her mind.

Julie received her allowances, but she really couldn't handle money. She would usually spend it all as soon as she got it and then be asking staff to 'lend us a few bob to buy me fags'. We found out that she had always wanted a leather jacket. Near to Mildmay there was a wholesaler who sold leather jackets and so Shirley, our counsellor, paid him a visit. She told him we had a patient who was very sick, who had wanted a leather jacket all her life – could he help? He told us to bring her over. So Shirley took her to see him, with her £50 clothing allowance.

'How much have you got luv?' he asked her. '£50,' said Julie.

'OK, have a look round and see if there's anything you like.'

As it was a wholesale warehouse, the individual garments

were not marked with the price, but it was clear the one that Julie had selected was one of the best there.

'How much is this then?' she said.

'Is that the one you like, the one you want?' he replied. 'It's £50 to you!'

As she was wheeled into the ward, Julie had a grin from ear to ear and apart from when she was in bed she always wore her leather coat, whether it was hot or cold. She had enjoyed going out to buy the coat and as a result went on visits to Camden Market, the local flower market in Columbia Road, Petticoat Lane and even Southend for the day. Everyone who went with her to Southend said they had all had a lovely time, but when I asked Julie she replied, 'No – bleedin' 'orrible!'

As her condition deteriorated, her fear of being alone extended to a fear of dying alone and of falling asleep and never waking up again. As a result she became, at one time, frightened of going to sleep unless someone was holding her hand. Unlike the early Julie we knew, she now loved to be held. She had learned how to love and be loved.

She had also become friendly with our chaplain and one day she told him she would like to know about 'religion' – was it too late for her? He reassured her that it was not and that God loved her. She said to him, 'Will you say a prayer for me, but not that "Our Father" thing' (her early experiences of a father figure had been so traumatic that to her 'father' equalled 'bad news'). From that time onwards, Peter and many of the staff would pray with her at her request and gradually she would join in herself. In an atmosphere of love and security, Julie was free to share her fears and pain, but it was in her own time and at her initiation.

Two months after her admission, her general condition started to deteriorate quite rapidly. She had been getting weaker for days, had become incontinent of urine, and complained of severe abdominal pains and headache. She was diagnosed as having a chronic aseptic meningitis, probably due to HIV. During this time she put many of her personal affairs in order. As she neared the end of her life she asked Shirley to write to her son for her. He was now eight years old and she wanted the adoption society to give his parents the letter for him for when he came of age. It was a heartbreaking letter for Julie to write, and in it she told him a little about herself, and the fact that she was going to die, but above all she wanted him to know that she had never forgotten him or stopped loving him.

She would often ask us to read Psalm 23, which she loved, because she thought of Jesus as the Shepherd and of herself as a lamb. Jesus became real to her and over this period her fears gradually disappeared and she became peaceful. She asked me one day, 'What do you think is going to happen to me when I die?'

'I think you are going to be with Jesus,' I replied, 'and if you can think of the most wonderful place and time in your life, then I can tell you that I believe that being with Him is going to be even better.'

Julie said, 'This is the best home I've ever 'ad, you know, it really is.' She asked to see Peter and talked with him and Shirley about her funeral service. She chose the hymns she wanted and the reading, which was to be Psalm 23. She did not want the Lord's Prayer to be said.

Ten weeks after Julie was admitted to Hospital, she died, having been deeply unconscious for several days. Mildmay had become her home and the staff her family. Apart from her girl friend she had no one, and so it seemed fitting that her funeral took place at Mildmay.

Moving on

As the months passed we found ourselves in a position where all our beds were full and there were more patients to be admitted than we could accommodate. During 1986 the possibility had been considered of using Tankerville Ward on the second floor to provide single room units for young disabled patients. (Tankerville had been partially refurbished at the same time as the work on Elizabeth Ward was carried out.) It was proving very difficult, however, to obtain sufficient funding from the Social Services to enable us to provide a standard of care of equal quality to that provided for our patients with AIDS. The authorities were just not willing, or able, to increase the funding even to match inflation, and their payments were months in arrears, which was causing us serious cash flow problems. We were already having to subsidise the existing facilities heavily and this in turn caused problems in funding the GP beds, which were funded from voluntary donations. It was clear that we were going to be unable to increase the accommodation for young disabled people.

We then began to consider seriously the possibility of using the second floor for more accommodation for people with AIDS. AIDS money at that time was 'ringfenced' and under the direct control of the Department of Health. We had successfully negotiated for revenue funding with the Department for the first nine beds, and so we went to talk with them about the increasing demand for our services and the possibility of them providing the revenue for us to open further beds. We would provide the capital to refurbish Tankerville Ward and our initial plan was to provide six twin and two single rooms. Many meetings and negotiations took place following this initial consultation. As a result the Department of Health agreed to provide revenue support for an additional eight beds.

At the same time, in consultation with our patients, we were made increasingly aware of the benefit that a day centre could provide in terms of supporting patients and carers, and enabling people with AIDS to remain longer in their own homes. Many patients told us how isolated they were, and how they longed to meet in a social setting with other people in a similar situation. They wanted an opportunity to discuss things openly about their illness that had to be kept a secret from most of their acquaintances. If we were to open a further eight beds at one end of Tankerville Ward, we would have a large open space at the other end which might serve well as a day centre. We therefore instructed an architect to draw up some provisional plans for us, which we discussed with patients, carers, and key members of the AIDS team in the Department of Health.

Our other patients

The fact that at that time we were not only caring for people with AIDS affected us both positively and negatively. On the positive side it was good to be able to demonstrate that people with AIDS could be cared for and integrated with other client groups and that our young chronic sick and GP patients were accepting towards the patients with AIDS, mixing freely with them in a social context. This was clear for all to see and was far more effective in breaking down fear and prejudice than words ever could have been.

On the negative side, however, compared to the money available for AIDS care, there was a lack of funding which meant we were not able to provide an equally high standard of service to the patients on Mathieson Ward. Although we were constantly refurbishing and upgrading Mathieson, we did not have the gifts of furnishings and equipment which had been donated for Elizabeth Ward and, when I took visitors from one ward to another, I was very aware of the difference. Much as we would have liked to, we simply did not have the voluntary funding to provide the same standard of care. In fact, by now, we were becoming increasingly concerned that the majority of our voluntary funding intended for capital refurbishment was needed to subsidise the revenue budget for Mathieson Ward.

Hope and high standards

Despite the worries over the care of our non-AIDS patients, there was so much to be excited about and we knew we were making good progress in many areas. Our emphasis on the best possible standards of care certainly had much to do with the early growth of our AIDS work.

One of the issues we had spent a considerable time discussing was how we would present hospice care to young people in such a way that they would not be put off from using Mildmay's services. Hospices are seen by some as places where you go when 'nothing more can be done'. In fact, I was asked by one young man, 'Is it going to be tender loving care and nothing much else provided by a group of do-gooders? Because if it is, I don't want it. I don't want people giving up on me, I don't want ever to be told that nothing more can be done. I can't live without hope, and I can't go into a place where I know the only way I'll come out is "feet first".'

From the earliest days of our planning we had known how important it would be to have care of the highest standard given by properly qualified professionals. It was also vital that we offered hope, in practical ways wherever possible. One thing I know now is that there is always something that can be done for our patients. We quickly found out when admitting patients that for them all, the hospice could not be a place they only went to when acute treatment was no longer an option. We had to establish strong links with the acute centres who were referring our patients, to ensure their quick return to the acute centre should they require diagnostic facilities, or should an acute regime need to be initiated. Whilst we would maintain treatments at Mildmay, we did not have on-site diagnostic facilities and could not initiate acute treatment. Patients who were referred for respite and rehabilitative care were still under the control of the consultant at their acute centre. The medical care of those referred for terminal care, however, became the responsibility of the Mildmay medical staff.

Once the ward was open, the pattern of referrals assisted us in a practical way. Whilst we had originally set up a unit for terminal care which also offered respite and rehabilitative beds, the terminal care element of the work actually only accounted for 40 per cent of referrals. The other 60 per cent were for respite and rehabilitative care and therefore we had evidence that most of our patients improved during their stay with us and returned home feeling much better. Word about this quickly got round to potential users of our services and our referral rate continued to increase rapidly. We also believed that if the care we offered was clearly high quality and responsive to need, patient directed and flexible, then the patients themselves would actively want to come to Mildmay to be cared for.

It may be that one day we will only have sufficient beds to be able to cater for the needs of the terminally ill. However, I think we were right in thinking that a reputation for high professional care will attract referrals for respite and rehabilitative care as well. The hope and high standards we offered certainly did encourage people to come to us and helped them overcome any reluctance they may have had to be admitted to a hospice. After all, our emphasis was on *living*, not dying.

4
A TIME OF GROWTH
1989

The most important thing

Living . . . I remember one of our early patients, a very attractive young man of twenty-two called Thomas. As a result of his HIV disease he was somewhat uninhibited and childlike in his ways. He would go round saying to staff and other patients, 'I love you, do you love me?' He would also say to anyone, 'I have AIDS you know,' in a very matter-of-fact way. He enjoyed working with the counsellor and during one session he drew a rainbow.

'There's one thing missing though,' he said.

'And what's that?' asked the counsellor.

'A crock of gold.'

'And what would you do with a crock of gold?'

'I would spend it,' replied Thomas.

'What would you spend it on?'

'Life.'

Thomas died two weeks later.

Tankerville Ward

Life at Mildmay at that time meant a great deal of planning. It was very hectic during the next few months. We received a request from the Department of Health (Architects department) asking us if they could evaluate the accommodation we provided for people with AIDS on Elizabeth Ward. They wanted to do this because, if they were asked to design accommodation in the future, they would be greatly helped by information gleaned from evaluating our project. We felt the information might help us too, and they carried out the evaluation over a period of several weeks. One of the main points to emerge was that patients strongly preferred single rooms and would have been reluctant to share.

Other providers in London at the time had planned to have shared rooms because patients had said that they did not want to feel isolated and lonely, and that they liked someone to be with them for company. These were valid reasons, but the Department of Health's evaluation at Mildmay confirmed what we had discovered when speaking to patients at the planning stages of Elizabeth Ward. I remember speaking to one middle-aged gentleman who was being cared for in an open ward in a major London hospital. He said to me, 'It's so terribly embarrassing to have diarrhoea such as I have and to have to use a bedpan with only a curtain separating you from the next patient. It strips me of any shreds of dignity that I might have left.' It seemed that privacy and dignity were of paramount concern: companionship could be provided in other ways.

These discoveries meant that we had to look again at our plans for Tankerville Ward, because we had originally proposed to have six shared rooms. The Board had by now agreed that Tankerville Ward should also be used for people with AIDS, and detailed plans were therefore drawn up for eight single rooms at one end of Tankerville. Final refurbishment work started at the beginning of 1989.

It was planned that the Day Centre would occupy the other, open end of the ward, but first, preliminary impressions regarding the need for day care had to be confirmed. In the spring of 1989, therefore, a Senior Nurse was appointed to research the need not only to provide day centre facilities, but also a home care service. During the next few months she visited day centres and home care services in cancer hospices as well as HIV community care teams. She talked to people with AIDS, their families and friends, and also primary care teams. Following that, plans were formulated for our own services.

As the bills started to come in for the refurbishment work,

we found to our horror that, as for the Elizabeth Ward refurbishment, the actual costs were way over the original estimate. As a result Mildmay accumulated a deficit of £300,000. The refurbishment work was stopped, all development plans put on hold and a day of prayer was organised as a matter of urgency. During that day our Chairman had a meeting at North West Thames Regional Health Authority which she could not change. Whilst we were praying at Mildmay, she told them of our needs. They said they would give £150,000 if North East Thames Region would give the same amount. But, replied Mrs Taylor Thompson, what if North East Region would not match the offer: then Mildmay would have nothing. Following negotiations, North West Region agreed to give us the £150,000 unconditionally. On leaving that office Mrs Taylor Thompson contacted North East Thames Region, who did agree to match the amount given by North West Region. So, amazingly, we had our £300,000, and the work could go ahead. Staff were still praying when the Chairman returned and told us the good news. This was one of many instances when God performed miracles to resource the work at Mildmay. It was the first and only time we asked the NHS to provide capital funding.

The Princess of Wales

On 14th February 1989 we received a telephone call from Buckingham Palace. They had a request to make. Would it be possible for the Princess of Wales to visit Mildmay on 24th February? She would come for one and a half hours and would like to visit the wards and meet patients and staff.

We were thrilled to grant the request but with only ten days' notice to arrange a royal visit we had to get moving! I quickly drew up a programme for the visit and sent it to the Palace by return of post. A couple of days later, staff from the Palace, including a security officer, visited Mildmay to be shown the route for Her Royal Highness's tour. The programme was approved and arrangements made with a Palace rota for press coverage. Patients were invited to bring in their relatives and friends and were asked if they would like to meet the Princess. Most said that they would, provided there was no camera coverage.

As soon as it was known that the Princess of Wales was going to visit Mildmay, her visit became the main topic of conversation on Elizabeth Ward. Simon, a thirty-four-year-old man with very advanced disease, asked his nurse if he could give Her Royal Highness a bunch of flowers; not only that, he wanted to give them to her in public in front of the photographers and television crews. The nurse had to point out what it might mean for him to go public as a person with AIDS. One of our patients had been on television at Mildmay's official opening and had subsequently received some abuse and distressing hate mail. 'I know all about that,' said Simon, 'but it's what I want to do. I have a special reason, you see. I'm desperate to find my family, and if by going on television I might achieve that, I'll do it.'

Simon had been in Mildmay for several weeks. He had advanced Kaposi's sarcoma affecting his skin and lungs, which meant he had dark purple blotches and generalised swelling all over his face and body. He had been given medication and physiotherapy to give him relief from the oedema (swelling) and it had improved. Nonetheless, when he woke up in the mornings he was unable to open his eyes, but as he got up and the day went on, the swelling would reduce and he would be able to wear his bright red spectacles again. He had difficulty in breathing following exertion, but although his condition was deteriorating rapidly, he still remained cheerful and able to enjoy his life. The sadness for him was that he received very few visitors. He had lost contact with his family four years previously. Following a row, he had moved away and then they had moved also. He had written several letters to them, but these had been returned with 'unknown at this address' written on the envelope.

When Simon came to Mildmay he described himself as being a lapsed Catholic, mainly, as he said, 'because of conflict between my lifestyle and my faith'. He said this part of his life needed dealing with and asked if he could see the Catholic priest. He met him on many occasions and seemed to find comfort from their interactions. He gradually refound his faith and his peace of mind was evident to all those caring for him. The priest gave him Holy Communion at his bedside which meant a great deal to Simon. He said it was the first time he had felt close to God for many years.

It was agreed that Simon would present Princess Diana with a bouquet and from that time onwards over the next week he could talk and think of nothing else. He decided he was going to buy some new clothes to wear for the occasion and asked his nurse to go out with him in the hospital transport to help him choose his new gear. They went out for several hours and although Simon was extremely tired, he was so happy and excited. He would not let anybody see what he had bought. 'It's a surprise,' he said, 'and I want to have maximum impact.' He also went and had his hair cut and his beard trimmed.

The day before the visit, a man from the BBC rang me up and said, 'I understand that you are having a person with AIDS going public tomorrow? I just wanted to check that you have explained to him what the possible implications are of him doing that. Much as we want to feature him, there have been incidents of persecution of these patients following exposure.' I thanked him and assured him that we had spoken to Simon, but that I would do so again.

I went to see him and told him that the BBC had rung me, and that they wanted him to know the score. 'Whatever it costs, if this will put me in contact with my family, I am prepared to pay the price. I haven't got long now and they don't even know I'm ill, let alone dying. I know they wouldn't deliberately turn their backs on me now, they just don't know where I am and what I'm doing. So it's OK, Ruth, please don't stop me from doing it. It's going to be the most wonderful day of my life, especially if I find my mum.' Simon looked at me through his red glasses, his eyes full of tears, as he said, 'I have reconciliation with God, all I need now is reconciliation with my family, and then I am ready to go.'

Friday 24th February arrived, a lovely sunny day, and Mildmay was the place to be that morning. The sniffer dogs were brought in to check the building over, and found themselves treated as celebrities in their own right by all dog lovers at the hospital. When their search was completed, the entrances to the building were searched and guarded.

On Elizabeth Ward Simon was getting ready. He had hardly been able to sleep the night before, he was so excited. He was helped to have a shower and dressed in his new clothes. When he entered the lounge he was given 'a right royal welcome' as he showed off his colour co-ordinated outfit. 'Just a minute while I do a twirl,' he said. 'How about the hair, the beard, do you like my aftershave?' He laughed and joked with everyone.

The Princess brought smiles to everyone as she entered Mildmay. The royal occasion, which happily coincided with our AIDS hospice's first birthday celebrations, also provided a special opportunity for the patients on Mathieson Ward as well as Elizabeth to meet the Princess. Clusters of balloons proclaiming 'We are One' had been placed around the lounge in Elizabeth Ward. They acted as a reminder that the hospice was exactly one year old and that everyone was united, body, mind and soul, in celebrating the fact. We were so happy to have the Princess celebrating with us.

After meeting the President, Chairman, and members of the Board, Her Royal Highness had coffee with us during a briefing by the Chairman, the Medical Director and myself. She then toured the wards and departments and met staff at every door and corner and groups of patients in the day rooms. She also visited patients who were very sick and unable to leave their rooms. Their nurses introduced them and then left the room, enabling the Princess to talk to each person privately. She sat on their beds and held their hands, which was seen as a gesture of acceptance and understanding. She had already done, and was continuing to do, so much by example to allay fears about social contact with people with AIDS.

When the Princess reached the lounge, Simon stood up and proudly presented her with a bouquet of spring flowers. She sat down with him. 'I really like your red spectacles,' she said.

'Not bad, are they?' he replied. 'Fifteen quid down Camden Market, do you want some?'

They laughed together, but as they chatted, Simon strongly underlined the fact that even in a hospice setting Mildmay's emphasis was really on living. He told her, 'I came to Mildmay for peace of mind, and that is exactly what I got. The people here care about me and care for me. They give me a quality of life and dignity which I could not have had elsewhere.' He said of Mildmay staff in a television interview later on: 'These people have given me back the will to live. That is the greatest gift that anyone can give.'

As the Princess went out of the doors at the end of her visit, a cheer went up from the many local residents who had come out to see her. She was given more flowers and as she left we realised just how much pleasure she had given to the people she had met and those who had just seen her.

Perhaps the crowning glory of her visit came later that day, however. On the evening news programmes of both BBC and ITV Simon's picture appeared in the item about the royal visit to Mildmay. He was being interviewed and spoke of his hope that he would find his mother. Within thirty minutes of the broadcast, Simon's family contacted Mildmay. They immediately set out to visit him and never left his side until he died peacefully ten days later.

Shortly after her visit to us the Princess was guest of honour at a royal film premiere organised by the AIDS Crisis Trust to benefit Mildmay. Thanks to the generosity of many supporters and famous personalities, the evening was a resounding success. Mildmay received £100,000 from the proceeds to go towards the cost of setting up Tankerville Ward.

Soon after Simon's death we received a framed photograph of Her Royal Highness and Simon with the inscription, 'To Simon, thank you for my beautiful flowers, Diana'. Sadly we had to inform her that Simon had already died. The Princess wrote back to say that we should send the photograph to Simon's mother, and she sent us another one to put up on the ward.

The day centre and home support service

A further substantial gift in June 1989 enabled Mildmay to press on with essential developments a little earlier than envisaged. Following the needs assessment carried out by the Senior Nurse, a day centre was being equipped and staffed to provide support for people with AIDS living at home. This would enable them to stay at home as long as possible, and also give much needed relief to carers.

Mr Greville Mitchell, founder of the Andrew Mitchell Christian Charitable Trust, donated to us a custom-built minibus-cum-ambulance, which was much needed to transport patients on the wards as well as those going to and from the day centre.

The day centre was planned to provide the following:

- social and diversional activities
- physio-, occupational, and art therapy
- hairdressing, dental services and chiropody
- intravenous infusions for maintenance and palliative therapies
- medical and emotional support and care
- nursing care
- advice on social problems

The need for a home support service was also researched at the same time and the following was recommended in the report:

That a team of community nurses from Mildmay supported by the Medical Director be set up. They will offer specialist medical and nursing care and advice and psychological support. They will co-operate with the statutory services in the area in providing a 24 hour service for the patients and carers at home. This facility will enable people with AIDS to remain at home, if that is their wish, even when they are very weak and ill.

Leading the way

The expansion of the work doubled the number of staff employed, and the need for continuing education for our staff resulted in the appointment of a tutor who would head up the newly formed Education Department. Demand for our educational services was continuing to grow, although we already had a programme for six seminars a year, residential work placements, open afternoons and training for volunteers. Following his appointment, the tutor received approval for the setting up of the English National Board 934 Course in 'The Care and Management of People with AIDS'. This meant that Mildmay was officially approved as a centre for post basic nurse education.

On 21st June 1989 Mildmay was mentioned as the national model for AIDS hospice care. The unqualified praise came in a major report for the government on AIDS by the House of Commons Social Services Committee. The Committee strongly urged the government to take 'an active expansionist role' in ensuring that similar hospices to the one at Mildmay were established in order to meet the increasing demand for this type of service.

Six weeks later a visit by the Prime Minister, Mrs Margaret Thatcher, confirmed this recommendation. She came unofficially on her day off, with no publicity, and spent the whole morning with us. She toured each ward and listened to a detailed account of the hospital's work, meeting staff and many of the patients. She had never been to an AIDS unit before and was very moved by the experience.

Time out for celebration

We had another cause for celebration when Professor Ian McColl, who was Head of Surgery at Guy's Hospital and President of Mildmay at the time, was made a life peer in the Queen's Birthday Honours List. He became Professor Lord McColl of Dulwich.

We continued to celebrate as old acquaintances were renewed and new friendships formed at a reunion in June. Two hundred and fifty old and current members of staff had the opportunity to reminisce and rejoice over Mildmay's history and future. Some ex-members of staff who attended had been at Mildmay in the 1930s. Scenes, events and personalities unfolded once again before their eyes as a presentation of archive slides took them on a trip down memory lane and through the years to the current day. Lunch and afternoon tea was provided in the Baptist Church Hall adjacent to Mildmay, and the conversation flowed as freely as the cream over the mountains of strawberries we enjoyed. The old and new staff compared notes and shared experiences. It was 'just like going home', said one 1930s nurse, 'except that I never really felt I had been away'.

Further plans

We were now seeing, for the first time, mothers with AIDS who had young children. They were finding that it was too much to cope with to have to care for children and do the household work when they were suffering from the physical and emotional exhaustion that is common in AIDS. Two rooms were therefore set aside on Tankerville Ward to enable mothers with children under five years to be admitted together yet with separate facilities. This made Mildmay one of the first specialist centres in the country to offer palliative care facilities for the whole family when one or more members of the family are affected by AIDS.

We continued to explore with paediatric centres and hospitals the particular needs of sick children with AIDS, and began to plan to provide further specialist facilities at Mildmay for children and families.

At the same time plans for a conservatory, to be sited on Elizabeth Ward's roof garden, were also under way. The conservatory was to be a focal point for patients from all three wards and it was planned that it would be a beautiful place with plants, flowers, hanging baskets and cascading water from a small fountain. The project was to be funded by the charity Crusaid.

The old casualty operating theatre at Mildmay was also dismantled in 1989 and converted, under the direction of the Medical Director and the Chaplain, into a chapel to provide patients, visitors and staff alike with a focus for worship and a place of tranquillity for reflection and meditation. One of Mildmay's supporters offered to design, make and donate a stained-glass window for the chapel. It was to feature the tree of life with the words, 'I am the Resurrection and the Life'.

Other visitors during that hectic year included Cardinal Basil Hume, Mrs Billy Graham, Lord Longford, and the musicians Marilyn Baker and Gloria Gaynor, who both gave concerts at Mildmay.

An emerging strategy

As the AIDS epidemic grew, the need for services to expand in response to this growth was evident. We had been planning our services since the beginning of 1987 and I believe our response was timely and appropriate. Following that initial decision to care for people with AIDS at Mildmay, we continued to be pro-active in the development of our strategies and in the search for further knowledge about the exact needs of patients.

Whilst we had set up a terminal care facility or hospice, we did not see this as being a better alternative to caring for people in their own home. We saw it rather as a support to community care. As such, the elements of respite and rehabilitative care were very important in enabling patients to remain in their homes for as long as possible during the course of their illness.

Respite care, where patients are admitted from the community to Mildmay, was often needed for patients who were living and coping alone and needed a break and a rest to enable them to continue doing so. Alternatively, it could provide the essential break that a carer needed to enable them to continue caring.

Rehabilitative care, on the other hand, was offered for

patients admitted to Mildmay from hospitals. This care was usually given to people who, having had a serious infection or illness, had received treatment but were too weak or incapacitated to return immediately from the hospital to their homes. During their stay at Mildmay they would be rehabilitated by receiving input from the interdisciplinary team as required, with the aim of promoting independence and a confident return to their home. Mildmay's care did not stop there. It continued into the community through the provision of input, if required, from the Mildmay Home Care Team and the offer of a place in Mildmay's Day Care Centre. We were assuming at that time that, if patients could be supported in the community, they would, generally speaking, prefer to stay at home.

Our initial support for community care had expanded enormously, especially in the last year. Since starting out, we had been on a steep learning curve: there was so much to learn about this new arena of care. We were also learning how the prejudice and stigma associated with this disease could create problems and complications. It made us realise that if it was difficult for us, it must be far harder for our patients. The small, but increasing, numbers of women coming to us were bringing with them a whole new set of problems.

Most of the women had small children for whom they were caring, and most of them were on their own without a partner. The facility on Tankerville Ward which enabled mothers to have their small children accompany them for an admission had been developed in an effort to respond to an urgent need, but it was clear that this arrangement was not ideal. A ward full of adults who were very sick was not the best place for young children. The situation of these mothers was further complicated by their fear that anyone would discover they had AIDS. If they had felt able to tell more people I am sure that others would have understood more of the situation from their perspective and would have demonstrated compassion instead of condemnation. But these mothers had no voice because they could not dare to be identified for fear of the effect it would have on their children, especially those attending school.

When they attended the day centre with their children it was obvious that if the mothers were going to have time to rest and relax, someone else would have to take care of the children. And so in the planning of future services for Mildmay we realised that we had to consider as a matter of importance the special needs of mothers with HIV and AIDS and their children.

Taking stock

The end of October 1989 had seen the eagerly-awaited opening of the eight beds on Tankerville Ward, the day centre and the home care service. As the year drew to a close with so much achieved, it was time to take stock.

Less than two years from the opening of the first four beds on Elizabeth Ward we had:

- opened the other five rooms on the first ward
- refurbished and opened a further eight-bed unit (we now had a total of seventeen residential beds)
- opened the Day Care Centre
- set up the Home Care Service Team
- set up the Education Department and appointed a tutor as head of that department
- seen a deficit of £300,000 eliminated overnight
- been enabled by unexpected major donations to proceed with developments
- been nominated as the UK model of AIDS hospice care

We were all very conscious of our need of God's guidance and wisdom as we developed Mildmay's services. It would have been frightening to take on these responsibilities without the knowledge that God was guiding us and would provide for Mildmay's needs. Many times He required us to take steps of faith, and to onlookers it may well have seemed that we were being extremely irresponsible, but our confidence was in God and in the repeated evidence we had of His goodness to us. We had much to be thankful for.

5

A TIME TO PAUSE AND A TIME TO REFLECT
1990

Consolidating activities

When services are expanded there is often a slow take up at the beginning, but we found this was not the case when we opened the extra beds on Tankerville Ward. Within a few months there was great pressure on the beds, with occupancy levels always exceeding 90 per cent. This in turn placed a great deal of pressure on the clinical staff because, often within an hour of a patient being discharged from a room, the next patient was being admitted. However, the excitement of new developments and the provision of a service they could be proud of helped the staff to cope with the difficulties. It was clear that we needed more beds, but we felt that we should pause for a few months and consolidate our existing residential services.

Within the hospital other developments and services were also moving ahead. Staffing in the education department had increased and the training remit expanded. A comprehensive programme of in-house training for staff was now offered to assist with essential training needs and personal developments. The seminars proved to be very successful and were mostly over-subscribed. There were seminars for nurses, doctors and church leaders, covering such topics as the care and management of people with AIDS, bereavement and loss, counselling and pastoral care. People came from all over the country, and also from Europe and other parts of the world, to attend the open afternoons and to meet members of the interdisciplinary team.

The media also showed a great interest in Mildmay's work

and came up with many proposals for documentary programmes. The common factor was that they always wanted to film, talk to, interview and sometimes confront patients. Many were surprised that we were unwilling even to consider their proposals. Our patients had come to us to be cared for and as well as this responsibility of care we quickly learned that they also needed protecting from the media. They were not to be treated like goldfish in bowls or animals in a zoo, there to be peered at by curious people, or filmed or photographed. Confidentiality had to be absolute. The fact that we lost numerous opportunities to raise the profile of Mildmay, to create awareness of its existence and its services, was insignificant compared to our duty of care to our patients. At this time, most of our patients were terrified of cameras and of allowing their HIV status to become public knowledge. A few people who had 'gone public' had experienced persecution and had been abused as a result.

Many people offered their services as volunteers. They were carefully interviewed, selected and trained to work on the wards. Their contribution was invaluable because they had the time to do all the little extras that contributed to the pleasure of the patient. They would sit with patients, read stories, play games and often do a lot of listening. They would also take patients shopping, or go shopping for them, or take them to the theatre, to hospital appointments, or simply go for a walk with them. Some of our patients had very few visitors, so the volunteers became important friends, vital members of the Mildmay family.

The counselling and welfare team were busy as well. Emotional support and family therapy was being given to an increasing number of patients and their loved ones. A need had been identified for a support group for the partners of patients who had died, and as a result a group was formed and met regularly one evening a month. Advice on social problems including housing and finance was greatly needed by our patients and the Welfare Officer worked long hours, often way into the evenings, trying to sort out problems for our patients.

We had managed to find the money to upgrade Mathieson Ward, the home of our young disabled patients, and they were now delighted with the improvements to their living accommodation and facilities. In came new decor, a new shower room, improved toilet facilities, new carpets and new furniture for everyone, and out went many patients in the customised minibus-cum-ambulance. Whether it was to the Barbican for tea, Wimbledon for tennis or to countless concerts, patients were happy to return to Mildmay at the end of the day. During the year, Mathieson residents often met up with the patients on the AIDS unit for barbecues and parties. This meant a lot to both groups, who were sadly accustomed to stigma and prejudice from able-bodied and healthy people.

The opening of the roof garden conservatory on Elizabeth Ward had created a place of beauty and a focus for social activity. The barbecue area on the roof had been retained so that patients could enjoy the sunshine while enjoying some food. One of our patients at that time was a florist and he donated some barrels which he filled with beautiful plants. Although the original plants were different, the barrels are still full of flowers today. They are a constant pleasure and a reminder of that lovely man. To be able to create such a beautiful haven in East London amidst so much dereliction and ugliness was very special and so much appreciated by our patients and their families. The plants and water and the fish swimming serenely in their large tank all spoke of life, peace and tranquillity.

Spiritual care

When the work to convert the old casualty theatre into a multipurpose chapel had been completed, it was consecrated in a commissioning service conducted by Bishop Jim Thompson who was then Bishop of Stepney. It was described as being a source of inspiration, a haven of rest and a forum for praise, and visitors to the chapel remarked on the unexpected pleasure of coming across the stained-glass window in such a modern setting. Again the emphasis was on life, with the text on the window reading, 'I am the Resurrection and the Life'. The chapel became the home of staff prayers, which took place every morning at 8.45 a.m. for fifteen minutes. During that time patients and their families would be prayed for and every day a different department of the hospital would be remembered in prayer, the staff members being mentioned by name.

We were becoming increasingly aware of the need of our patients for spiritual care. When people near the end of their lives they often have unfinished business with which they need to deal and questions to which they need answers. If we are to provide good quality of life in terminal care, then conflict, anxiety and fear must be addressed if they become evident. The control of distressing physical symptoms is not enough when patients also have emotional or spiritual pain, or anxiety about social problems. Questions commonly asked include, 'What will happen to me when I die?' 'How will I die?' 'Why me? I'm too young!' Fears are also expressed: 'I'm frightened of dying'. 'I'm frightened of death'. 'I'm frightened of hell'. On top of these, many of our AIDS patients are troubled about the way they have led their lives. Some feel guilty, some feel angry and others find that the only way they can cope is to deny the reality of the situation.

We found that spiritual pain (however that may be defined by the patient) is very real for AIDS patients and it was important that they could seek help knowing they would not be ridiculed or judged by their carers. The counselling and pastoral care teams would play an essential role in the holistic care of the patients and their families. Friends and families of patients need care too and often practical assistance to help them face distressing prejudice.

When I was managing community nursing in Southend Health Authority we had our first AIDS patient being cared for at home. I talked to the nurse caring for this patient and his family and suggested to her that when he died she ring the funeral directors herself and arrange for the body to be removed, because as the body would be in a plastic body bag, they might be reluctant to be involved, and I did not want the mother to experience this rejection. When the patient died, the nurse did as I suggested and arranged for the undertaker, explaining to him that the body would have a 'risk of infection' label.

She then had a cup of tea with the family and left. Thirty minutes after she left, the mother received a call from the funeral director and she was asked this question: 'Did your son have AIDS?' She was overwhelmed, but did not answer. He then said, 'Well, if you can't tell me he didn't, then he must have. I'm afraid we are unable to help you, you will have to find someone else.' Even today there are crematoria where staff are unwilling to deal with the bodies if they know the person had AIDS.

I tell this story because it is significant in explaining why so many families have asked us to contact the funeral director and want our chaplaincy team to conduct the funerals.

Knowing this need for spiritual care, Mildmay was busy strengthening its Christian witness through the work of the chaplain and through the development of worship and prayer opportunities for staff and patients alike. The patients' participation in the short services was entirely voluntary. Staff would join patients for Communion services where the one cup was shared by all. This was particularly significant for people with AIDS, who could be reassured by the way they were treated that they were not modern-day lepers.

The pastoral and chaplaincy work was increasing and requests were received for adult baptism and confirmation services to take place in the chapel. Requests to the chaplain to conduct funeral services and special services of remembrance were also on the increase and he was involved in training volunteers in the aftercare of bereaved families.

Although Mildmay was a Christian organisation, we respected the faiths, or lack of faith, of all those we cared for and the chaplaincy team was there to respond to spiritual needs as defined by the patients themselves. Some patients approaching death needed so much to experience reconciliation with family, friends and, for some, reconciliation with God. As our chaplain said one day, 'Perhaps one of my most moving experiences was to witness the peace in the face of a young man who decided to attend an Easter service on one of the AIDS wards and then found faith in Christ.'

In the course of our work with the families of patients it became clear to us that many of the parents who were evangelical Christians had real problems coming to terms with the homosexuality of their sons. At that time I had been asked to do a series of Bible readings in a book called *Lent for Busy People*. I had been asked to do a section on myself and another on care of people with AIDS at Mildmay. The section on AIDS included some comments about acceptance and non-judgmental attitudes. As a result of this a lady wrote to me saying that both she and her husband were Christians and they had a son who was gay. She had been so surprised, yet really relieved, to read of a Christian dealing with the matter with such compassion and understanding. She said that if there were any way in which she could help she would be happy to do so.

A vision formed in my mind of starting a support group for the Christian parents of gay men and women. I felt that I could probably ask Jean and her husband to assist with it, and wrote to her suggesting this. She was overjoyed, feeling it would be of great benefit if they could meet other parents in similar situations. I therefore advertised in the Christian press, asking anyone who was interested in joining the group to contact me in confidence. Twelve people wrote to me from all parts of the country, as far afield as Scotland, Devon and the Midlands.

Leaders of secular support groups wrote to me asking why I was segregating Christians and why I felt that they could not attend existing groups. I responded by saying that I had first-hand experience with these parents and had found that they often had particular problems which would be best dealt with in a group where people shared and understood the same beliefs and faith.

I managed to get some money from a charity to enable me to pay the fares of these families so that they could meet four times a year at my home. Two of my colleagues who worked with me at Mildmay came to the group as facilitators and later on, as more men came along, we were joined by Mildmay's chaplain. The average attendance at the group was ten, and people found great support in sharing their fears, anxieties and problems openly, the first time many of them had done so. They were at different stages along the road to understanding and acceptance of their son's lifestyle; some wanted to pretend it was not true, some were praying for a miracle to change him, but none wanted to lose the love of their son and the relationship with him. With the support of each other they found new understanding and ways of coping with the situation. Some of the young men even wrote to the group thanking them for supporting their parents in a very difficult situation. The group still tries to meet together once a year and it is always a very supportive and happy occasion.

Management

The growth of the services at Mildmay was resulting in increasing general management responsibilities. The medical work had also increased greatly. I was therefore invited to become the General Manager/Director of Nursing instead of Matron, while Veronica Moss, as Medical Director and the only 'doctor in the house', would retain only responsibility for planning and new developments. I accepted this new responsibility, provided the Board would enable me to undertake management training. The Board agreed to this and paid for me to attend the Senior Managers' Development Programme at the Kings' Fund College.

With the additional responsibility came the realisation that if you want to be popular you should not become a manager! 'You cannot please all the people all the time' was something that I found to be very true. In my previous work with the Southend Health Authority I felt that I was valued and respected by my staff as a good manager. Here at Mildmay, a Christian organisation, I found it difficult to cope with what I felt was constant criticism. Looking back, I can see that my perception was distorted and it was in fact the comments of one or two vocal people who made me feel that they spoke for the whole organisation. I decided that one way of dealing with this situation would be to find out more about myself, the things that made me angry, my emotional responses, my attitudes and prejudices. I therefore also undertook a two-year, part-time course on counselling skills and attitudes at Westminster Pastoral Centre. I found this to be extremely beneficial. I learned how to deal with anger and defensiveness in myself and how to respond to negative criticism and injustices. I am certainly not saying that I have all the answers, but with God's help I certainly learned how to cope with situations that I had previously found upsetting.

Funding

Despite the higher income being generated through grants and donations, this was being absorbed in total by the commitment to refurbishment, development and expansion. Independence as a hospital had brought with it loss of crown immunity and Mildmay had been forced to spend an additional £1.25 million on improving the hospital's facilities in order to meet the stringent requirements for voluntary registration, while also providing a comfortable, home-like environment. Mildmay had made contractual arrangements with the four Thames Regional Health Authorities and also applied for government funding and various grants as appropriate. The tremendous difference between what Mildmay received and what it needed to spend had to be found from the private sector, i.e. corporate and individual donations and independent fundraising. The need to bid annually for funding because longer-term contracts were not given was, of course, a concern. It was sad that a hospital as unique as Mildmay, and one so courageous and far sighted in its AIDS care, should have to fight a constant battle for financial survival. But we were not alone in that fight, and we were constantly grateful for God's provision for our work.

Mothers and children

Despite the constant strain of funding and the efforts involved
in providing all the services we had established so far, we were
strongly aware that there was so much more to do. As I
mentioned in the previous chapter, the needs of mothers and
their children continued to concern us. Whilst only small
numbers were presenting to us for care at that stage, we needed
to find out more about their needs in order to plan ahead. And
so it was that Veronica Moss, Mrs Taylor Thompson and I
were sponsored to visit New York, where many women and
children with AIDS were being cared for.

It was wonderful, the way God provided for our visit. At a
recent conference Mrs Taylor Thompson, our Chairman, had
made friends with a lady from New York called Mrs O'Mara,
who had said that if there was any way she could help with
Mildmay's work in the future we should let her know. That is
not the sort of thing you say to Mrs Taylor Thompson unless
you really mean it! Mrs O'Mara did mean it and during our
stay in New York she provided us with accommodation in her
own home and arranged for her brother to transport us
everywhere in his limousine.

During the year one of our visitors had been Princess Margaret. We had told her of our plans to visit New York and she
said, 'You must meet my friend, Judy Peabody. She is involved
in AIDS projects. I am sure she would help you to arrange your
visit. I suggest you ring her, and I will tell her to expect your
call.' The next morning I had a call from the Palace to give me
the telephone number and to tell me that Princess Margaret had
already contacted Mrs Peabody about us. Judy Peabody turned
out to be an amazing lady. She was a great benefactor of many
AIDS projects in New York and was therefore known by, and
had access to, all the major centres caring for people with AIDS.
She not only arranged our itinerary, but accompanied us on
most of our visits. We were always made to feel very welcome
and it was obvious that Judy was greatly respected.

During our ten-day stay we visited general hospitals with

services for women with HIV and AIDS, paediatric centres caring for children with AIDS, and many voluntary initiatives. The thing that stood out for me was the fact that many mothers were dying in acute hospitals whilst their children were dying in other hospitals and there was no way that this separation could be prevented. In effect, they were having no opportunity to say any goodbyes. I had taken with me a proposal for our unit at Mildmay, where families would be cared for together if one or more family members were dying, but I had not expected the response I got when I talked to people about it. They wept openly and I was told, 'We are having to do the best we can in the face of an overwhelming crisis and we are just having to react; you are so lucky; you have time – time to plan.'

Joey's story

It did not take much to see that the problem was far bigger than the facilities available. One encounter particularly brought the desperation of the situation home to me. As I entered the foyer of the large Paediatric Hospital on the first day of my visit to New York, there seemed to be mothers, fathers and children everywhere, sitting on the stairs and floor, and leaning against the walls. The toilets were locked up as a result of constant vandalism and if you needed to use the toilet you had to go to the reception desk and ask for the key. Soap and toilet paper were luxuries that were not provided here.

We took the lift with Judy Peabody to the second floor to meet the Director of Paediatric Services. She was a very large lady with a larger than life personality, and was sitting behind her desk with a pint of Coke, eating a Big Mac and chips and smoking a cigarette. She rose to greet us and we all sat down while she told us of the hospital's work with children who had AIDS. The hospital cared for children with all medical and surgical conditions. 'But the children in the AIDS ward break my heart,' she said. 'Many of them are orphans, their parents having died of AIDS, others are too much for the mother to handle and all of them have been abandoned. No one comes to see them; in fact we're their family, the only people they've got. What you're going to see is going to upset you, because you'll think, "they're just like animals in cages", but we do the best we can, given the money and resources we have.'

She obviously cared passionately about these children and told us how all her staff collected the freebies from hotels and free samples from stores, packets of sugar and salt from the burger houses, unwanted gifts – anything that could be given to mothers in the AIDS clinic to attract them to return for their appointments. When they came they would be able to take a handful of the goodies from the big basket in which they were kept.

As the Director continued to talk about the AIDS crisis, as she called it, her eyes filled with tears. She told us that she had a rule in the paediatric AIDS wards and it was this, 'Every member of staff must pick up and cuddle each child on their ward twice a day. At least that way, they will get a little physical comfort and stimulation, but it's not enough.'

When we arrived on the first ward I could understand why she had said the children were like animals in cages. The ward was full of row after row of metal cots, all with the rails up and clear plastic canopies covering the tops. The babies and small children lying in these cots were quiet and still – there was hardly any noise in the ward. They were all spotlessly clean, with dry nappies and bedding. When I picked up one of the babies she did not respond when I talked to her and held her, in fact, she appeared not to respond to any sort of stimulation. She was living but not alive.

My attention was then taken by a little boy who was moving around in his cot. He was trying to reach a bottle of milk on a locker near the cot. I asked the nurse if he could have it and she said, 'Yes,' but I could not pass it through the rails of the cot as they were too close together. The boy was sitting in the cot in a white nightie, with strings tied at the back of his neck and around his waist. I unhooked the canopy and he took the bottle, but just sat with it in his hands. We talked to him and he showed no response. He just stared at us, his face and large

brown eyes showing no emotion. His name was Joey and he
was two years old. He was small for his age, but he did not
look particularly ill. We were told his mother had died and
because he was HIV positive, and there was nowhere else for
him to go, he had been brought to the ward. Although he had
been ill he was not ill at present.

I wanted to know the full story of this lonely child. Joey was
the only child of an Hispanic mother. They lived in the Harlem
district with her mother, her sisters and brothers and two of her
sister's children. Joey's mother Maria had started using drugs
when she was fourteen years old. She became a prostitute and
worked under the control of a pimp in order to fund her drug
habit. She had shared works with other drug users and had also
been at risk of infection through unprotected sex with numerous
partners. She gave birth to Joey when she was seventeen years
old and shortly after that she became sick with a chest infection
and was diagnosed as being HIV positive, and later as having
AIDS. Her mother tried to look after her and the baby as best
she could, but there was very little money in the house, and
Maria and Joey were malnourished and unkempt. Maria had
pneumocystis carinii pneumonia but was reluctant to go into
hospital for treatment because that would mean leaving Joey.
She did not have money to buy the things she needed for herself
and Joey, and she was very anxious and frightened.

She wrapped Joey up and took him and all his belongings in
a box to the hospital. She had to make sure he would be taken
care of. The social worker admitted Joey to the ward and
immediately arranged for Maria to be admitted to the District
General Hospital, but it was too late for Maria. Her condition
deteriorated over the next few days. She died when she was
only nineteen years old.

So what of Joey? What kind of life had he had up until now?
Certainly his mother had loved him and had cared for him to
the best of her ability, but with inadequate housing, food and
clothing, life was difficult. Often she had been under the
influence of drugs, almost unaware of his needs, and at other
times she had been too ill and weak to be able to do much for

him. The guilt that she felt must have been overwhelming: 'He has no father and no proper home. I am a junkie and he is infected because of me. He is going to be an orphan because of me and he is going to die because of me.' I was told that this guilt prevents many mothers like Maria coming forward with their children for care and treatment.

As I left the ward I could not get the picture and the story of Joey out of my mind. We all felt a deep sadness and a heaviness of heart for this little boy. Little did I know that ten days later I would meet Joey again, but in very different circumstances. We had arranged to visit a centre for 'boarder babies'. This was a place where children who were known to be HIV positive were cared for pending fostering or adoption (although we were told that adoption was almost impossible for these children as people were not willing to take them).

As we entered the building we realised immediately that it was different from the other places we had visited. There was the sound of laughter and children's voices – happy sounds. We were told that each of the children had his or her own designated care attendant, and there were nurses on duty and a full-time Medical Officer on call at all times. We were taken to the children's bedrooms, which had lovely bright colours, pictures on the walls, mobiles hanging from the ceiling and plenty of toys everywhere. The nursery had large slides, play houses, bicycles and scooters and an outside play area. The children were being cared for well and the staff gave them many hugs and other expressions of love and affection.

Suddenly a little boy caught my eye. He was wearing a bright yellow suit and was pushing a baby walker. I looked at his dark brown hair and big brown eyes and realised that it was Joey! Gone was the little face devoid of all expression and in its place was the face of a little boy who was interested in, and responding to, everything and everyone around him. He had been in there just over a week. They said that when he came he was quiet and unresponsive, but even over those few days he had changed amazingly. He could not talk much, but he could understand what you said to him. His nurse said to him,

'Where's Joey's bed?' and he pointed to his bedroom. I stretched out my arms to see if he would come to me and he did. As I held him, I marvelled at the way in which he had changed. Now he was responding to love and care and was being stimulated by his new environment.

Joey was one of the fortunate ones, and they told me he would probably soon be fostered. I remembered the others back in that silent hospital ward and realised how easy it would be to be overwhelmed by the complexity and size of the problem in New York. But there was hope: Joey proved it. How privileged the staff of that centre were to be able to change the life of even one small boy who had been brought to them in such great need.

Learning from New York

What had we learnt that would benefit us and prepare us for the plans we wanted to make at Mildmay? There was much to take into consideration.

I had a real sense that it was as though this tragedy had insidiously crept up on people unawares in New York. Now it was too big for their resources. I was so glad that we had realised the potential problems that could be developing for mothers before it was too late for us to be able to respond adequately. I spoke to doctors who said, 'Five years ago we could see that we were going to have problems of the type we now have, but five years ago when there were only comparatively few women and children who were sick, we were laughed at and rebuked for being alarmist.' It was hard to witness their despair as they told us these things. 'We can only do our best day by day to respond to the problem, but by 1991 it is estimated that there will be 20,000 AIDS orphans in New York State.'

We were told that mothers were presenting too late for treatment because of their responsibilities to their family. In a study carried out in 1990 by the Paros Institute, called *Triple Jeopardy, Women and AIDS*, it was reported that mothers delay in presenting themselves for care and it was found that on average there were only forty-five days between mothers presenting for care and their death. What could we do to prevent such a situation developing in Britain?

Back at Mildmay after our visit to New York, we invited women who had AIDS to take part in our discussions and these 'consumers' were involved in the planning and development of our new service. Their input was essential and we had realised how easy it is for health care professionals and planners of care services to think they know all the answers. If we could only start off on the right track, not only would our service be more cost-effective, but it would also mean that we would be meeting the real needs straight away, rather than wasting time changing direction while the problems escalated unanswered. The challenge of helping these women and children might turn out to be Mildmay's toughest yet.

Telling the story of Joey and his mother Maria, I touched on the guilt which many mothers say they experience. I think it is quite impossible for those of us who are not affected to comprehend the enormity of this problem. Many of the women are from backgrounds where movement into the world of prostitution, drugs, poverty and disease seems to be an inevitable progression. I know from my own experience that children who have been abused carry an enormous burden of guilt which stays with them into their adult life. As adults we can look at this and say, it's not the child that should feel guilty: it's the abuser, it's the people who treated the child so badly. So we then ask the question, 'Whose guilt is it?' Sometimes we can follow that through and find out that the abuser was abused and so it goes on.

These young mothers seem from some perspectives to have made many wrong choices. But why? Their experiences will have informed those choices, and affected their ability to make the right choices. These experiences may have included the encouragement to use drugs to 'improve' the quality of their lives, then the addiction that resulted from the drug use, then the prostitution and theft necessary to finance the illegal drug habit and then the progression from pill popping to intravenous drug use.

Then, faced with AIDS and imminent death, their thoughts must run along the same lines as Maria's did: 'I shouldn't have used drugs, especially IV drugs, and I shouldn't have shared works. I shouldn't have slept around, not for money, not without protection. I'm a junkie, a prostitute, a thief and now I have a baby. I'm not looking after him properly. He hasn't got a father, a family who care about him, enough food or proper clothes. I'm going to leave him. I'm going to die. He will be an orphan and he will suffer and die and it's all because of me.'

On top of this burden of guilt come anxieties about confidentiality, because of the stigma and prejudice caused by a diagnosis of HIV and AIDS. This is true in every part of the world. Mothers will often not come forward for treatment and will not identify their child as being in need because of the perceived guilt and stigma of AIDS.

Is it any wonder that some of these mothers feel worthless, useless, hopeless and wish they had the courage of those who commit suicide? Others can only cope with life by shutting it all out, never addressing problems, taking more drugs and alcohol and living with denial as their coping mechanism. What could Mildmay do to help them out of this desperation?

We believed then, and still do, that with care and support these mothers can be helped to face life and to discard inappropriate guilt, to forgive themselves and others and get on with living. When we were planning the Family Care Centre, we made sure that the mothers who were helping us knew that they were of great value and that they were making a very real contribution to the future care of families. Looking back now, I can say that the care God led us to develop for families has turned hopelessness into hope for many mothers.

6

A TIME TO MAKE CHANGES
1991

The closure of Mathieson Ward

After years of being one of the few local providers of long-term
residential care for young chronically sick and disabled people,
Mathieson Ward was to close. We had been experiencing
persistent problems in recruiting staff to work on the ward. At
that time trained nurses were in short supply, therefore nurses
could choose where they wanted to work and few chose to
work with the type of patient for whom we were caring on
Mathieson Ward. The work was heavy and repetitive and
patients did not get better. The only staff who stayed for any
length of time were those who came with a sense of vocation.
We had to appoint agency nurses to cover the shifts and this
resulted in soaring costs for nursing and in a turnover of nurses
which prevented continuity of care and was not conducive to
the patients' quality of life.

The situation had been further exacerbated by a lack of
statutory funding and an inability on Mildmay's part to continue subsidising the balance, which amounted to £275,000 per
year. As anyone involved in fundraising will know, people are
not interested in giving to running costs: they prefer to see
'bricks and mortar' as a result of their donations.

On top of all that, we were not happy with the way that we
were providing our care. The environment was too much like
hospital care, and money needed to be invested in converting
the facilities to ensure that the clients felt more as though they
were at home. They needed transport, money for social activities, and many of them needed more suitable clothing. This

would have meant an increase in the costs of the local authorities and, since they were not in any way funding existing costs, we realised it was going to be impossible to provide a service that was both appropriate to the patients' needs and one that we would be proud of.

The decision to close the ward came after much thought and prayer. Seven of the original residents had died or had been placed elsewhere and we now had to decide what we were going to do. If those original patients had still been with us, I think we could not have considered closing the ward, so we were helped by the fact that they were no longer with us. We spoke to the remaining residents and their families who were, of course, very upset. One wrote to the *Independent on Sunday*:

> After being shunted around hospitals and rehabilitation units, Bruno found what he needed at the Mildmay Mission Hospital in East London, with high-quality facilities and nursing care that included the extras essential to make institutional life acceptable. Art and music therapy were laid on, together with regular trips to the seaside, the theatre and the pub, and counselling and support for relatives.

The letter praised the hospital, said how much it was needed, and complained that it was forced to close.

In the same newspaper I described the whole thing as 'a wretched situation' and it was – wretched for the residents who had to move on, wretched for the twenty staff who had to be made redundant, and wretched for the Board and Management who were forced to make the decision. We believed, however, that it was the only course of action open for us, because if we had continued with mounting deficits we could have found ourselves having to close everything. We believe the closure of Mathieson was part of God's plan for Mildmay, however hard and painful it was at the time.

I was certainly heavy-hearted. When we set up the AIDS services in 1988 I felt it was good that Mildmay was not 'all AIDS'. The fact that Mildmay could demonstrate that people with AIDS did not need to be isolated from other patients was significant, especially at a time when there was so much fear and ignorance around. Our chronically sick and disabled patients and their families had expressed their willingness to be cared for alongside people with AIDS. They had still needed reassurance, certainly, but we had given that to the best of our ability. The evidence that it had been effective was to be found in the integration that subsequently took place between the two groups of patients, and this was remarkable and a joy to see.

There was one young girl called Susan who had become paralysed from the neck downwards as a result of surgery for a brain tumour. In her early twenties, she was not an easy person to care for, as she exhibited anger and aggression and at times simply refused to talk. Following one barbecue, one of the young men on the AIDS hospice ward, who was also paralysed, became a frequent visitor to her room. They were often to be found talking animatedly together. The young man went home following his admission for rehabilitation, but some months later was readmitted for terminal care. Susan found out that he had returned and would often take herself up to Elizabeth Ward and find her way in her wheelchair to his bedside. Like Susan he had no family, but there was always a nurse, volunteer or friend in his room, where he now lay unconscious. Without speaking to anyone, Susan would sit for hours beside his bed just holding his hand.

During the three years in which we had cared for the two groups of patients, at no time did we have any problems or demonstration of fear. The two groups seemed to have something to offer each other – they were both young, neither would get better, both had experienced profound losses, and these common factors resulted in a oneness in their time of need.

So when we had to close Mathieson Ward we felt that we had lost something very important. In the future the public would come to know that we only cared for people with AIDS, and that in itself could bring about problems for patients in terms of confidentiality of diagnosis.

It had to be done, however, and the staff at Mildmay set to

work to find new homes for our five remaining residents and to assist the staff who were being made redundant in finding new positions. This was achieved and several of the staff told us that from that situation God had opened for them wonderful new opportunities. 'Our disappointments are often His appointments.'

In view of increasing referrals for AIDS care the Board decided that we should refurbish Mathieson Ward to form an additional AIDS hospice and continuing care ward. It was established that Mildmay would need to raise £300,000 to cover the capital costs of refurbishment. We prayerfully considered plans and sought funding for this purpose. Our young chronically sick patients were no longer with us, but work had to go on.

The decision had been made earlier by the Board to rename Tankerville Ward and call it Alexandra Ward in honour of Princess Alexandra who had officially opened the new, independent Mildmay and Elizabeth Ward in 1988. It was therefore also decided to rename Mathieson Ward to celebrate the refurbishment, changing the name to Helen Ward in honour of Mrs Taylor Thompson. She had been awarded an MBE in the 1991 New Year's Honours List, in recognition of 'services to the public sector'. It was a well-deserved honour and everyone at Mildmay was very proud of her.

Helen Ward was to be a timely addition in view of the hospital's growing waiting list and an occupancy level which, despite the addition of the eight beds on Alexandra Ward, was again constantly exceeding 90 per cent. It was a while, however, before refurbishment work could actually be carried out.

VIP *visitors*

With the closure of Mathieson looming, we were very much in need of encouragement, and to the delight of the staff and patients, the Princess of Wales decided to visit Mildmay again in 1991. In the privacy of their own rooms, patients told an attentive Princess how they coped with their condition and how they found the strength to carry on. Words of comfort were in turn offered by the Princess with real feeling and a sense of understanding. The conversations were always individualised, highlighting the ethos shared by Mildmay that every person counts. In the day centre she met several patients and sat with them, admiring some paintings which one of them had done. Such is the magnetism of the Princess's presence that what was a comparatively brief encounter for some will remain imprinted in their minds for a lifetime. Patients were unanimous in describing her visit as therapeutic and uplifting. 'She filled the place with warm smiles and happy hearts,' said one patient.

One particular person she met during her visit was Michael Kelly, who had been a patient and was then a volunteer at Mildmay. Michael had done much for Mildmay and for people with AIDS, raising money and awareness by being featured extensively on television and in the newspapers. He gave the Princess some flowers and they spent a long time chatting. He said afterwards, 'Meeting the Princess of Wales in the place which cared for me and taught me how to live again has to be the greatest honour I could have wished for.'

The Princess had requested that she be kept personally informed of the developments at Mildmay and she saw the architect's drawings for the Mother and Baby Unit. She asked us to continue to keep her informed.

We had many other important visitors during that year, including the Duchess of York. She lost no time in commenting on the extraordinary atmosphere of the place. She said she felt so comfortable and relaxed in the warm, caring environment. Her own warmth and spontaneity was greatly appreciated by all the patients, some of whom she saw privately in their own rooms. She went from ward to ward and also visited the day centre, where she met sixty-three-year-old Joe. He enjoyed a dubious reputation among Mildmay's staff, especially for refusing all offers to clean up his permanently dirty glasses. The Duchess spotted Joe peering at her through these glasses and promptly declared, 'You can't see me properly; I would love to give your glasses a quick wash.' Before Joe could protest, she took them from him, washed them in the adjoining treatment room, dried them with a paper towel and placed them back on his face. 'Here you go, Joe, can you see me now?' He had to agree that his view of the Duchess was much improved.

Another celebrity to become involved with Mildmay was Cliff Richard. He held 'An Evening with Cliff Richard' at the Duke of York's Barracks in Chelsea, which was a dinner and cabaret in support of Mildmay's AIDS Unit. Prior to the evening Cliff and his manager visited Mildmay and went on a tour of the wards, meeting patients and staff. During the evening he expressed his open admiration for Mildmay, for its Christian vision and inspirational lead in AIDS hospice care. Between songs Cliff spoke with warmth, conviction and often humour about his Christian faith and lifestyle.

We were also honoured by church dignitaries, receiving visits from Dr George Carey, Archbishop of Canterbury, accompanied by his wife Eileen, and from Cardinal Basil Hume. Dr Carey and his wife, who is a nurse, chatted to many patients on the wards. Those who met him remarked on his friendly manner and general concern for those living with the disease. One patient commented, 'Many people with AIDS are too frightened to admit their diagnosis; the Church should be the one place where there is no fear of rejection.'

Cardinal Hume came to open a new guest suite for the families of patients being cared for at Mildmay. In London accommodation is scarce and costs are prohibitive. If a loved one is ill and dying, family need to remain close, but the last thing they want to do is to spend time trying to find somewhere to stay. Cardinal Hume had launched a fundraising appeal and with the money raised, we had been able to convert part of the hospital's nursing accommodation into three large, self-contained apartments for patients, friends and relatives. Designed particularly with long-distance visitors in mind, the suite had been attractively and comfortably furnished to cater for up to six people. Before officially opening the suite in September, Cardinal Hume offered up a prayer of dedication: 'It has been a great privilege to be personally involved with this project, and I hope and pray that all those who stay here will find peace, comfort and reassurance during the times of anxieties and sadness.'

Support also came from members of the cast of *Eastenders*. June Brown, who played the part of Dot Cotton, was guest of honour at an auction for Mildmay and Todd Carty, who plays the character of Mark, a person with HIV, visited Mildmay. Todd met patients who had developed the virus in real life when he spent a morning at Mildmay. It was his first visit to an AIDS centre. 'While playing the part of Mark,' he said, 'I have come to know a lot about HIV and AIDS and can really empathise with some of the problems faced by those living with the disease for real.' Our patients were in fact very impressed with the actor's sensitivity and understanding of the whole subject of AIDS as they discussed with him some of the issues and challenges they faced. Todd said that he hoped this interaction would help him further in his screen role.

Financial provision

Our success in obtaining funding for our AIDS services from the NHS brought with it a responsibility to be professional on the business as well as the clinical side of our work. We already had a reputation for providing high quality professional care to our patients, but the situation on the administrative and financial fronts was giving us cause for concern. We had very poor financial information and were unable to resource this side of the work in the way that was becoming increasingly necessary. Interestingly enough, looking back, we can now see that if we had known accurately how unstable the financial situation of Mildmay was, we would never have dared to proceed with developments. I sometimes wonder if God protected us from that knowledge on purpose!

We decided to 'buy in' some expertise and so appointed CASPE Consultancy Services Ltd to work with us to produce our first business plan. In order to do this they had to obtain as much financial information as they could. They found that at certain times, such as in the middle of the month, we some-times did not have sufficient funds to meet the salary require-ments of staff, who were paid at the end of the month, but that by the time salaries were due, the money had always been there. They also found that we had embarked on major capital projects with very little money in hand, but that by the time the money was needed it had always been supplied. In the letter that accompanied the business plan, the consultant wrote, 'The faith of these people is mind blowing!' He did highlight the very real need to appoint a qualified accountant to head up the finance department. The reason we had not appointed one before was that we were all on charity salaries and the Board felt we could not afford one. As General Manager, I was earning 20 per cent less than we would have had to pay a qualified accountant. Following the report, the Board reviewed the salaries of the hospital management team and we decided to advertise for an accountant at the appropriate salary. We had a good response and were successful in appointing David Rouse as Director of Finance. From that day on things have never looked back in the Finance Department and we are grateful to God for this.

The consultant from CASPE had also been requested to look at projections for women and children with AIDS in the UK, with a view to conducting a feasibility study into the provision of services for families. The indications from that survey were that by 1994 there would be a need for such services.

Meeting the needs of mothers

We were certainly beginning to get more requests from mothers with babies or young children who needed to be admitted for respite and rehabilitative care. The two large rooms on Tanker-ville Ward were big enough to take a bed and a cot, but we realised it was difficult for a mother to rest if she had to entertain and care for her child all the time. We managed to raise the money to buy nursery nurse cover for the duration of the mother's stay in Mildmay, but the problem of entertaining the children, particularly in wet weather, still needed to be resolved.

We had a room near the ward that we thought could be used as a playroom and made a bid for £4,000 to the BBC Children in Need Appeal to refurbish and equip it. We were delighted to be successful in our bid and a bright, colourful and well-equipped nursery was soon created. Mothers could now be admitted for respite care and could relax in the knowledge that their children were just a few yards away, well looked after. One mother said of her child: 'Jennie may be a bit of a handful sometimes, but I couldn't bear to be separated from her at this time. If she had had to go into care I couldn't have come in.'

The nursery was to have another significant part to play in the care of mothers in the day centre. We had listened to the needs expressed by current female patients as well as support groups such as Positively Women, and we decided to provide a Women's Only Day once a week at the day centre. On that day, the room became a crèche facility with trained nursery nurses kindly funded by Barnardos. The playroom was invaluable and much appreciated by the mothers and their children.

One factor in the decision on the Women's Only Day was that many of the women attending the day centre were of African origin, and some were finding it very difficult to talk about personal issues in front of men, because within their culture this was just not something that was acceptable. The need to talk about things that really concerned and worried them could not be ignored. If we were to provide a caring environment for them we were bound to respond to that need by creating an environment where women would feel free to talk about personal problems, women's issues and things that they found very upsetting. With a Women's Only Day, their children would be cared for in the crèche whilst they could focus on the things that they liked doing and needed to say.

The idea turned out to be a great success. One popular activity was to cook a variety of foods for each other. Matoke with groundnut sauce and chicken was the favourite! As many of the women were mothers, they also had the opportunity to talk about their children and the problems they were encountering with them. Having said that, I never found the atmosphere heavy, rather it was always a happy place to be, with lots of laughter, singing and a wonderful smell of the day's special dish! Any excuse for a party would do, despite the very real and painful problems faced by these women.

Millie's story

One day two of the ladies who attended the day centre asked if they could see me in my office. As they came in I could see immediately that they were very nervous and upset. I had met them before and they had told me that they had come from Uganda to settle in Britain. In both cases their husbands had died of AIDS and they were left alone to care for their children. Mary had two teenaged daughters and Millie had one little girl called Prossy (short for Proscovia), who was seven years old.

Millie had told me of her anxieties about Prossy's future. Her daughter had lived in Britain all her life, and so to return to Uganda to the care of her extended family would be transporting her into a completely different world. 'I find it hard to talk about the future,' she said, 'but I know that I have to make plans to ensure that Prossy will be taken care of properly. Talking of her future when I am not here serves to remind me, and bring home to me so much that I am going to die, but I just have to do it. When my husband was ill we had to keep quiet about what he had and especially not let Prossy know in case she talked to anyone about it. I feel I can't talk to her about my situation, I can't bring myself to burden her with all my worries. For the moment I tell myself she is better not knowing. We get on as best as we can. I come to the day centre and in the school holidays she comes with me. The one thing I am thankful about is that she has not got the virus.'

I remembered these things as I sat facing Mary and Millie, and asked them how I could help them. 'Well,' Millie started, 'It's the green ambulance, you see. The one you collect us in and take us home in.'

'Yes, I know,' I said, encouraging her to go on.

'Well,' she faltered and Mary took up the story. 'We wondered if you would remove the name "Mildmay" which is painted on it.'

'I'll tell you what happened,' resumed Millie. 'The bus took me home from the day centre and as I got out of the bus I noticed that the lady in the flat above me was looking out of the window. I went inside, put my things down, got Prossy's skipping rope and went out again to meet Prossy from school and as I did I noticed she was still there, watching.

'I picked Prossy up and she skipped happily alongside me. As we neared the flat I got my key out of my purse and walked up the path towards the door. As we did so, I heard Prossy scream out and I saw the lady in the flat above disappearing inside and firmly closing the window. Prossy was crying and whimpering with shock. She was absolutely soaked from head to foot. This woman had thrown a bucket of water over her. I took Prossy inside and took off her wet clothes, bathed and put on clean clothes and comforted her.

'She asked me between her sobs why that lady had done that to her. I told her that some adults and some children do funny things sometimes, without any obvious reason. She said, "You go and tell that lady off, she mustn't do that to people." I couldn't tell her that I was too afraid to go upstairs and confront that lady. We lived there alone and I was sure that my neighbour already knew more about me than I wanted her to know. So I told Prossy that it was better not to fight with people who were like that because it only made things worse.

'I think the reason she did that, Ruth, was because Mildmay was written on the side of that green ambulance. She has seen me come back regularly and, because Mildmay was on the television when Princess Diana came, she and a lot of other people around here now know that Mildmay equals AIDS.'

I was deeply saddened by this story, and of course, immediately arranged for the name to be painted out on the ambulance.

Reasons for persecution

Why are people with AIDS and their families forced to live in fear of people finding out about the diagnosis? What prompted a woman to throw water over the child of a family she believed had AIDS? These problems are very common and sometimes I wonder if things are improving at all.

I would often sit in the day room, talking to the parents of patients, and one thing they had in common was the feeling that Mildmay was a safe place where they did not have to hide in a shroud of secrecy, and where they could talk about their real problems. Almost every person I talked to said that they had not told friends, or the community in which they lived, the real cause of the illness of their son or daughter. They would usually say that he or she had cancer and was in a London hospital. I asked them what they feared from telling their friends the truth. Their replies were similar:

'I'm afraid of their response, I think they will be horrified.'
'They wouldn't want to have anything more to do with us.
'They would say he had brought it on himself.'
'They would say that we as parents were to blame.'
'I fear rejection and isolation.'
'People would think bad things about my child.'
'I need compassion and understanding and I can't be sure I'll get it, so it's too risky to tell.'
'People don't understand; they are still frightened of catching it, even though they have been told they can't through social contact.'
'Because it's a terrible disease and there's no cure, people think it's best to keep right away from any perceived risk.'
'Some people think that anything to do with AIDS is perverted, sexually deviant and nasty; it's different from anything else in some people's eyes.'

To expose themselves to people who might be judgmental, repulsed, critical and lacking in compassion is understandably more than most of these families can risk. I met one set of parents whose son had been in a cancer hospice. Although they found that the staff were trained, very understanding and happy to care for their son, they were paralysed by fear. Their son was suffering from HIV dementia and he was uninhibited. He would go around saying to people, 'I have AIDS, did you know I have AIDS?' For that reason his mother and father were very reluctant to let him out of his room and into the patients' lounge or dining room, for fear of what he was going to say and the response he would get from the other patients. For their part, they did not want to mix with the patients or other visitors for fear they would be asked what was the matter with their son.

In order to be effective in fundraising, Mildmay's profile has to be raised in the public eye. It is necessary to give potential donors information about the organisation so that they can understand the work they might fund. We have had many opportunities for television and journalistic coverage, some of which, to the surprise of the media personnel, we have declined. Since we opened over seven years ago, hardly a month goes by when we do not receive a request for media coverage but, as I have said before, we have never been tempted to accept offers which will negatively affect our care for our patients. We will not ask patients to go in front of cameras, unless they wish to, because we understand perhaps more than they do what this could mean for them.

In the early days of the epidemic here in Britain there were some brave people who talked about their problems on camera. Many of these were persecuted as a result, their cars and homes being damaged, and one even had dog excreta put through the letter box. When I was speaking with a women's group in New York, they told me about one woman who had gone public and spoken on television. By the time she returned home, her flat was on fire.

So the dilemma still exists for us. As Millie had told me, 'Mildmay equals AIDS', and the more people who are aware of this, the greater the negative effect it has on our patients. It may be that even now some will not come to Mildmay to be cared for, because if their friends knew where they were, their secret would be out. Having said that, however, I hope I am right in thinking that, for those who come, enormous worth is discovered in the acceptance, love and high quality care available to patients and their families. At least, once within our walls, they can shed the cloak of secrecy and deal openly with the real problems.

7

A TIME TO BE CREATIVE
1991

Africa

That same year, 1991, also saw us forging important links in
Africa. The numbers of men and women of African origin
coming to us for care were increasing, and we noticed that there
were cultural differences that meant parts of our service were
insensitive to those patients' needs. It was decided therefore that
members of staff would bid for travel fellowships or bursaries
to enable them to undertake a study tour to Africa. I was
successful in being awarded the 1991 National Florence Nightingale Scholarship sponsored by The Smith & Nephew Foundation. Worth £3,000, the award enabled me to undertake an
eight-week study tour of Kenya, Uganda and Zimbabwe. The
purpose of the visit was to study resources and services available
for the care of people with advanced HIV and AIDS and issues
relating to the care of whole families, including the social and
cultural differences in the approach to AIDS and terminal care.
Dr Veronica Moss, our Medical Director, Shirley Lunn, the
Head of Counselling, and Sue Rouse, Head of the Home Care
Team, were also successful in obtaining funding to undertake
all or part of the study tour.

This was the first time I had visited a developing country and,
on the whole, I loved it, especially Uganda. In the hospitals we
visited we saw that people with AIDS were being cared for in
the general wards. In one country, however, we saw people
with AIDS on mattresses on the floor at one end of the ward.
We were told that the doctors had not been to see them because
they had nothing to give them. Drug treatments were in short

supply and the doctors could only give treatment to those who could be made better. We also visited paediatric and neo-natal wards, where we saw many ill children and babies who had been abandoned.

In Kenya we visited the Nairobi Hospice and went out with the nurses to see patients in their own homes. It gave us hope to see what was being done for cancer patients and I am sure that from that small beginning, palliative care will gradually be introduced more widely in Africa.

We had a few frightening experiences in Kenya and I record one in particular. We were to visit a World Vision project in a slum district just outside Nairobi. It was the time of a big rally in support of multi-party elections and feelings were running high. People had been warned to stay indoors on the day of the rally which was due to take place on the day after our visit. We had travelled on deeply pitted murram roads in a car with a local World Vision manager, a very intrepid lady. As we neared the site of the project, our car was surrounded by young men who tried to force the doors open. They were unable to do so and our escort managed to drive away. We visited the project, but had not been there long when we were asked to come outside. Some elderly ladies, who seemed very agitated, were speaking to the project managers in Swahili and making urgent signals which we understood to mean that we should go.

The managers were debating whether to put us straight back into the car in which we had come, or whether to wait for a bigger vehicle that was approaching from the other direction, as they would then be able to send some of the male staff to accompany us. The elderly ladies were becoming very anxious, however, so we were quickly whisked into the small saloon car in which we had come, with our lady guide as driver and a strong looking man who squashed in with us. He did not reassure us because he was clearly terrified himself. We locked the doors and windows and drove off. It was very difficult to manoeuvre the vehicle as the road was potholed, crowded and cars were blocking our way. Our driver managed to get through, only to find a little further on that there was a coach right across the road. The only possible way past was to drive round the end of the coach into the steep slope towards the ditch. It was not something that one would normally have risked for fear of turning the vehicle over, but when our driver saw the group of excited young men approaching us, she just put her foot down and off we went. It was by God's grace and mercy that we did not tip over and managed to escape.

The security problems in Kenya at that time were such that it was very frightening for someone who had never been to a developing country before. We were told, 'Don't wear gold necklaces and dangling earrings. If you do, don't leave the car window open, because when you stop a thief might pull them off your neck and ears. If somebody comes up to you with a gun and demands the car, don't look at him, just hand over the keys and get out.' There was also an embargo on the women of our party going out alone at night, and I was told of one British consultant who had set out from his hotel to go a few yards down the street to a meeting at another hotel. It was broad daylight, but by the time he reached the second hotel he was minus his suit, his shirt and his shoes! We were glad to be travelling on to Uganda!

As I became familiar with Uganda, I found it was a special place and I loved its people. They were so open and friendly. Whilst there, we visited AIDS clinics in government and non-governmental hospitals, health clinics in rural areas and we also went on visits with home care teams. We were privileged to travel south to Rakai district, which is one of the worst-hit districts in Uganda as far as AIDS is concerned. I was amazed to see the courage and resilience of the Ugandan people who had been through so much hardship over the years and were now confronted with the devastation that AIDS was bringing.

We went into poor homes where people did not have enough food, could not afford medicines or treatment, but were still trusting and praising God. Many families would ask us to pray with them, read the Bible and sometimes even sing a hymn. It was humbling to hear their thanks to God and to realise just how very little they had in comparison with us. What many of them did have was an unwavering faith that God was in control and would see them through. We saw orphans and their grandmothers who, in some cases, were caring for as many as twenty children. They were the children of their sons and daughters who had died of AIDS. It was easy to feel over-whelmed with the size of the problem: at that time in Uganda there were 30,190 people with AIDS, an estimated one million people thought to be HIV positive, and between twenty and thirty thousand orphans.

Becoming overwhelmed was not an option, however, or it would have been too easy to give up and feel that the situation was hopeless. As we met and made contact for the first time with people in Uganda, and as we talked to nurses and doctors during our stay, we did not know what wonderful opportunities God was to open up for us in that beautiful country in the years to come.

While we were visiting and learning from projects in Africa we were also asked to speak and teach at government and non-governmental hospitals and voluntary organisations. One of the people we met in Nairobi was Mr Malcolm McNeil, Regional Manager for East and Central Africa for the Overseas Development Administration (ODA). He asked if we might be interested in conducting AIDS training courses for trainers, initially in Kenya, Uganda and Tanzania. I said that we would certainly be very interested and he invited us to submit an outline training proposal. Little did we realise at the time where this would lead. On our return to the UK I submitted a proposal which was accepted, and the first two courses were planned, to be held in Kenya in 1992. This was to be the beginning of our work with the ODA and the British Council.

When the Princess of Wales had last visited us, we had told her about the proposed study tour of Africa and she had asked us to keep her updated, so we sent her a copy of the report we had written, which had included some photographs taken on our visits. You can imagine our delight when we received an invitation for Mrs Taylor Thompson, Dr Moss and myself to take coffee with the Princess at Kensington Palace and to tell her about our visit. We took a set of slides and a map of our route to show her, and we spent over an hour talking with her and answering her questions about the AIDS situation in Africa. The Princess was clearly very interested and it was obvious that she had read our report with considerable attention. We told her that one day we hoped she would go to this part of Africa, to show her love and concern for the people with AIDS there, as she had done in the UK, to touch and hold them and demonstrate that people with AIDS were not to be treated as untouchables. I still hope that one day she will come to Africa with us.

Advice to Poland

At about this time we also received an urgent call for help from medical and nursing staff at the Suwalki General Hospital in Poland. The government there had realised that, although numbers of patients were relatively low at that time, they must plan to make provision for the care of people with AIDS. Health care professionals in general were unwilling to care for people with AIDS, and so it had been decided that every new hospital being built would be directed to make provision to care for these patients. As the staff in the Suwalki General Hospital were not happy to care for people with AIDS, a ten-bed specialist AIDS unit was to be set up in conjunction with the Drug Dependency Clinic in the psychiatric wing of the hospital. We were asked to visit the hospital in order to provide training for staff, and were happy to help.

When we arrived we realised that unfortunately the proposed AIDS unit was being set up in the secure section of the hospital, separated from the other facilities by locked doors. We started our workshops for staff and found that staff from the general hospital were also coming into the sessions. We were then asked to provide a day seminar to the staff in the general hospital. This was very well attended and we facilitated sessions on attitudes, prejudices, fears, and facts about transmission.

Following that visit, the Director of Psychiatric Services and the Chief Nurse in the Psychiatric Unit made a return visit to see Mildmay's facilities at first hand, and to undertake a three-week orientation and work placement programme. We learned later that as a result of our training and their return visit, people with AIDS were going to be nursed with other patients in the general hospital and that the secure psychiatric unit was not going to be used for them. We were satisfied that our efforts to share our experience and knowledge had been beneficial.

A publishing venture

By now, of course, we certainly did have considerable experience, and in our spare time, during the last half of 1990, Dr Veronica Moss, Mildmay's Medical Director, and I had been busy writing a book. Now published, it was on terminal care for people with AIDS, largely based on the Mildmay model. Veronica and I had worked together a great deal to develop Mildmay's services and it was a pleasure for us both to be able to work on something that would benefit many nurses and doctors as well as ultimately benefiting people with AIDS. In the foreword to the book, Professor Robert Pratt, Vice Principal/Head of Faculty of Continuing Education, Riverside College of Education, London, wrote, 'Like its authors, this book reflects love and hope and provides for the first time the expert guidance needed to be with our patients in a meaningful way as they confront the final stage of their lives.' Medical, nursing, counselling and social dimensions were also included, and our aim in writing the book was to improve the quality of life of patients, enabling and encouraging them to *live* with AIDS.

Centenary plans

It was a busy and demanding year, 1991, but we had much to look forward to as well: 1992 was to be Mildmay's centenary year, and on World AIDS Day, 1991, we were delighted to welcome the husband and wife team of Desmond Willcox and Esther Rantzen as joint patrons of the Hospital's Centenary Appeal. Due to be launched in 1992, the Appeal was to finance new capital developments, the first phase of which was to be the refurbishment of Mildmay's reception area, the building of the Family Care Centre and the purchase of land on Hackney Road in front of Mildmay. Further developments being considered at that time included a new education centre, new day and therapy facilities and a coffee shop for patients and staff.

Desmond Willcox had produced one of the first television documentaries on the AIDS epidemic in San Francisco, and had foretold the crisis that was to hit Europe. When he spoke on World AIDS Day 1991, he said, 'For the most disastrous and the most urgent reasons, the Mildmay Appeal is one that we must all pay attention to. AIDS is currently devastating many families and in one way or another is going to touch and hurt many thousands more. It cannot be ignored. We have to respond to the epidemic in our midst.'

Centenary logo

In preparation for the centenary year we decided that now was the time to introduce a new logo.

A firm of strategic design consultants kindly donated the new logo for use in the Centenary Appeal. The new design was chosen because it was felt that it depicted what Mildmay was all about. Telling comments included:

    'It's one person caring for another.'
    'It's two people in harmony.'
    'It's a mother and child.'
    'It's old and young.'
    'The contours look like flames of fire (or the Holy Spirit) rising out of Mildmay.'
    'It promotes well-being.'

'It's an image of hope and strength.'
'It signals acceptance.'

It seems appropriate therefore, to end this chapter with the story of Peter, a story about acceptance and the restoration of harmony to a suffering family.

Peter's story

Peter lived with his parents just outside London. When he became ill, he had privately consulted a doctor at a London teaching hospital and it was there he was diagnosed as being HIV positive and having AIDS. He had never consulted his GP, who was unaware of the situation, and so his mother had cared for him alone with no help whatsoever for three months. Peter had continued to be treated privately by the consultant as both he and his mother were terrified of anyone knowing his diagnosis. He had shared the information only with his mother – his father Harry and sister Wendy were unaware of the cause of his illness.

Over the months Peter had become increasingly unwell, suffering from short-term memory loss, weakness in his legs and incontinence. Caring for him was quite a struggle for Helen, his mother, as she was seventy-three years old and not in the best of health herself. The problems were compounded by the need she felt for secrecy and by the real fear she had that AIDS was easily transmitted. Since Peter had become ill, she had refused to allow her daughter to visit the family home as she was frightened that her grandchildren would catch AIDS. This had caused a great deal of misunderstanding and a family rift had followed. Peter's father Harry could not understand why Helen did not want anyone to visit the home: 'Why are you so stubborn? You're killing yourself. Let Anne next door help you, she's a trained social worker, she's used to dealing with people who are sick. Cancer is nothing to be ashamed of, and you are making him feel worse by isolating him and keeping everyone away.'

Little did Harry know that the last person Helen wanted in the house was Anne. She might put two and two together and start asking awkward questions. She had to admit to herself that Peter did look like those AIDS victims pictured on the front pages of the tabloid newspapers. And so Helen struggled on until Peter became really worried about his mother and, in response to questions from the social worker at the private hospital, he admitted that she did need help. The social worker suggested that he be admitted to Mildmay for a fortnight of respite care. Peter discussed this with his mother, who immediately denied that she needed a break. She said, 'I can look after you better than anyone else, I understand you,' but she thought, 'I can't face up to these people who know he has AIDS, I'm too ashamed, they will think I should have brought him earlier.'

Peter tried to persuade his mother to accept help, partly because he had had enough of being shut away from people and having no one to talk to except his mother and he had realised she did not want him to talk about negative things. In the end it was agreed that Peter would be admitted to Mildmay just for a weekend to give his mother a break.

She came with him to Mildmay, but when he was taken up to the ward she ran away. She returned to visit the next day, however, and managed to cope because the staff realised that she was apprehensive and fearful and that she needed space. This encouraged her and she started to relate to the staff, especially the chaplain and the counsellor. As the weekend drew to a close, Peter told his mother he wanted to stay longer and she did not oppose this, in fact she seemed quite relieved. Slowly Helen began to trust the staff and began to talk about her fears and what it was like for her to be in this situation. She really did need to talk and she told the staff what a relief it was to be able to talk openly with people who understood. 'I thought everybody would be very critical and judgmental about the situation and I thought it better to pretend that Peter had cancer because, what with his illness and everything else, I just couldn't cope with people being hostile and unkind.'

The time came when Peter and Helen both thought his father

Harry should know what the real situation was. Helen had managed to persuade him not to visit Peter in hospital because she said Peter was there to rest and not be disturbed. 'I only just sit there when I go; it will be a complete waste of your time, when he's bad and confused. I don't even think he knows that I am there.' And so Harry had stayed away.

Helen and Peter decided that the best way to inform Harry was for Helen to talk to him at home. The counsellor talked through with her how she thought she could break the news and this increased her confidence to face the task. She was able to tell Harry and to her amazement he said, 'I'm not surprised, I guessed it. He isn't getting any better is he? Don't you think I wondered why you didn't let the kids come round?' Harry asked if he could go and see Peter. 'Does he want me to come?' Helen reassured him that Peter had wanted his father to know and would certainly be wanting to see him.

In the meantime Wendy, Peter's sister, had contacted Mildmay. She was suspicious and had found out that her brother was having respite care. She suspected Peter had AIDS and she rang Mildmay asking if her brother was an inpatient and did he have AIDS? It was becoming increasingly difficult to consult Peter because of his dementia, and so the counsellor spoke to his parents about the need for his sister to know – for the sake of Peter, his sister, the grandchildren and themselves. They understood, and together the parents went to see Wendy and told her, then took her with them to Mildmay to see Peter. The family were reunited and now were in a position to support each other. Harry and Wendy realised that fear had totally paralysed Helen.

Peter was discharged home from Mildmay to be cared for by his family. The GP was informed and became involved in Peter's care. They were also supported well by the District Nurse and Mildmay's Home Care Sister. Wendy's children were able to visit their uncle and Peter was surrounded by people who loved him.

As Peter became terminally ill, Helen asked if he could be re-admitted to Mildmay. The family still wanted to be involved in his care, but he now needed twenty-four-hour nursing and medical care, and even with community support they felt inadequate and a little afraid. And so Peter came back to Mildmay for his last admission and Helen and Harry came too. They were able to stay in the Hume suite near to the ward. Peter only lived for a few days, but during that time Helen helped care for him, Harry supported her, and his sister and some of the community staff visited him. Helen and Harry were able to take breaks, but could still be nearby, knowing that Peter was not being left alone. The interdisciplinary team provided support and care to the whole family, which continued in the form of bereavement support after Peter had died. 'To be able to stay with him and yet at the same time be cared for myself was a wonderful experience, not just for me, but for the whole family,' said Helen.

8
A TIME TO CELEBRATE
1992

Looking back

The thrill of seeing dreams become reality at Mildmay must have been there for the deaconesses and other staff of the hospital a hundred years ago, just as it is for us today. The area in which the old hospital was sited was so noisy and filthy, and the living conditions so appalling, that it formed part of London County Council's first slum clearance scheme. The old hospital, with the adjacent slum dwellings and warehouses, was demolished.

In 1892, when they moved into the new and splendid red-brick, purpose-built hospital in Austin Street, the staff at Mildmay must have experienced the excitement of new beginnings and expansion, as we were doing exactly a century later. The Austin Street building had fifty beds, almost doubling the capacity of the old, 'disused warehouse' hospital.

The area around Austin Street was much quieter then, even quiet enough to hear the clip-clop of the horses' hooves as they clattered along the cobbled lane. One hundred years on, and celebrating our centenary year, we were reminded how much had changed with the passage of time. Despite the fact that the cobbles had only been covered less then five years previously, cars now brought so much noise and pollution to the area. The constant stream of traffic going to and from the city on the Hackney Road and the sudden, frequent screams of the police sirens, both day and night, shatter any tranquillity that might exist. The staff in 1892 would have been delighted to be moving to work in Austin Street, but not so the staff today: it is not one of our greatest privileges! In our centenary year, however, we wanted to concentrate on the positive things, and there was much to celebrate. It was also to be a year of hard work on the part of many people, which brought with it some marvellous achievements.

Appeal for funds

Our Centenary Appeal was duly launched in 1992, with Desmond Willcox and Esther Rantzen as patrons. The Appeal Committee was made up of volunteers who had fundraising experience, or who were influential in their social or business lives. We needed good leadership of the Committee, to ensure that the impetus of the launch was maintained with enthusiasm. Lady Gill Brentford was just the person to provide this. She set to work to develop and oversee the various committees in order to achieve our target of over £3 million for the first phase of a £10 million appeal.

At the same time as the voluntary funding for the capital costs was being sought, we were also trying to ensure that the running costs of the planned Family Care Centre would be affordable to the NHS. How could we do it? It was clear that caring for a mother and/or father with a child was going to cost more than caring for one individual. Fundraising for children (and animals) is usually easier than fundraising for any other group, so perhaps we could capitalise on that. The solution was to charge the same for a patient in the Family Care Centre as for a patient in any of the other three wards, and to fundraise for the extra costs.

We had already established contracts on the basis of the cost per day for one individual and, as the demand for beds was exceeding our ability to supply, we decided that we would apply in advance for the revenue funding needed for six extra beds from September 1993. We would raise the £100,000 needed to keep the children with their mothers from voluntary donations. We had cause to celebrate on both counts. The Regional Health Authority agreed to fund the extra six beds when they were opened and, within a short while, The Oak Trust donated the full £100,000 costs for the first year for the children.

With the growth of the organisation, the revenue budget for 1992/93 had risen to £3.4 million in total. Two thirds of the way through the year, however, Mildmay was owed over £300,000 by North East Thames Regional Health Authority, because they had run out of funds allocated to them by the Department of Health for AIDS care.

It was common knowledge at the time that North West Thames Regional Health Authority had a massive underspend of over £8 million. I was therefore extremely grateful when Virginia Bottomley, the Secretary of State for Health, agreed to see me, together with Veronica Moss, our Medical Director. We had collected data relating to the growth in demand for services in the two Thames Regions, especially North East Thames, and these statistics greatly supported our request that the allocation to North East Thames Regional Health Authority be increased so that essential services could receive adequate funding. I like to think that our meeting helped, for within two months the Region had paid off in full the monies owed to Mildmay and their allocation had been significantly increased for the following year.

Mildmay now had financial stability and we were confident of the funding for the next financial year. We were conscious of our responsibility not to be over ambitious at this time, but we certainly had cause to celebrate.

Apart from the Centenary Appeal, and our efforts to secure funds from other sources, individuals were also helping in the most remarkable ways. One of the problems facing disabled people being cared for in a building which is mostly a century old is that of independent access. As I have indicated earlier, the loss of dignity and self-esteem that can come from having to be dependent on others for basic needs is something that should be avoided whenever possible. The access for disabled people on the wards had been improved, and it now became obvious that wheelchair users could not operate the ancient and very heavy lift between floors for themselves.

Michael Kelly, one of our patients who was working as a volunteer at Mildmay, was particularly concerned about this. Together with Claire Wheatcroft, the Publicity Manager, he decided to launch the 'Give us a Lift' appeal for £35,000 to refurbish the old goods lift into one that could be operated by disabled people. They worked very hard to raise the money, and were helped by a substantial legacy, but the pleasure experienced by patients who no longer had to ask for help when using the lift made it well worth the effort. It was another cause to celebrate during that special year.

New-look Mathieson Ward

Mathieson Ward had lain empty, cold and padlocked for a year since we had been forced to close it due to funding difficulties. The pressure on our beds was continuing to increase and now was the time to act on the planned refurbishment of Mathieson Ward to provide more beds. We knew, however, that we must first obtain the agreement to expansion and increased revenue funding from the NHS.

An effective way to convince the authorities that the extra beds were needed would be, we felt, to enlist the support of the referring hospital doctors. They were very aware that demand for beds at Mildmay exceeded our ability to supply, because they were the ones whose beds were blocked. This was because priority was always given to patients who were terminally ill or those for whom care in the community had broken down. After all, in hospital they were already being cared for.

We wrote to the consultants of all the designated AIDS wards and other consultants caring for people with AIDS in London, asking if they would support the expansion of our residential service to twenty-eight beds. We explained that we would be sending any letters we received to the Minister of Health, with copies to the AIDS team in the Department of Health. We had a superb response. They all replied, supporting the expansion. A typical comment ran: 'If I am to care for the increasing numbers of patients needing acute care, I must be able to send patients to Mildmay as soon as they are ready to go. At present there are just not enough beds available. It is essential that Mildmay's residential service is expanded now.' The consultants also commented on the high quality of the service provided.

We sent the letters to the Minister, and shortly after that the revenue funding for the further eleven beds was agreed. Although the increase in the number of beds would mean that the unit cost per bed per day would be reduced, the wonderful thing for us was the willingness of the authorities to increase the overall allocation to Mildmay by a significant figure.

We could now go ahead with our plans to refurbish Mathieson Ward, and were determined to waste no time. All facilities were improved to the same high standard as the other two wards, with the capital costs funded by £300,000 from voluntary donations. Once the work was completed, we had a further eleven single rooms with en suite facilities. As planned, we could now give our new-look ward its new name of Helen Ward, after Mildmay's Chairman, Helen Taylor Thompson. It was marvellous to see the plans laid in 1991 come to fruition.

As was our custom now, prior to opening the new facilities we had a week of open days so that those making referrals and others could see where patients would be cared for. Once patients were admitted, of course, their need for privacy would be respected. As far as the staff were concerned the opening of Helen Ward could not have come soon enough. They were concerned because, already, they had occasionally had to turn a priority patient away. The increasing numbers of referrals we were receiving meant that the waiting list had often operated at double the number of rooms available. It was sad to have to realise, however, that while the new unit would certainly relieve pressure on Mildmay's existing programme, it would probably only provide temporary relief in a worsening AIDS situation.

A new uniform

While parts of the building were being overhauled, we also wondered if other things might benefit from a fresh look as well. We decided to conduct a survey to find out if patients still preferred the nurses to wear uniform. Over a period of time a questionnaire was designed and distributed to the patients and their visitors. The nurses were also invited to complete a questionnaire to let us know their views. The result was unanimous: the patients, their friends and families, and the nurses themselves, all felt that the nurses should be recognisable as such. The preference was that all other disciplines should not wear a uniform, with the exception of the physiotherapists. The reasons given by the patients were many and varied, and provided us with some fascinating insights:

'I find it easier to have personal things done for me by a nurse in uniform; somehow wearing the uniform gives them the right.'

'I can't see very clearly now, I have retinitis, but I can recognise the female nurses with the dark belt round their light dress and the male nurses by their white tunic.'

'It is important to me that I know who the nurses are. I get confused at times, but I always know the nurses by their uniforms.'

Over the next few months the nurses, both male and female, were given the opportunity to try out a number of different styles, for a week at a time, before selecting their new uniform.

Pastoral care and counselling

As the numbers of patients and their families for whom we were caring increased, so did the pressures on the pastoral care team. This year Nigel Schibild joined Peter Clarke to be the second full-time residential chaplain. He said that he had been attracted to Mildmay because he knew that people's spiritual needs were given high priority here. Right from the beginning of the AIDS work we found that the families and friends of many of our patients would establish a relationship with one of the chaplaincy team, whether they shared the Christian faith or not, and when their loved one died they would turn to the chaplaincy team for practical help or spiritual support. A substantial percentage of our patients also ask for pastoral care while they are with us, and some maintain contact after discharge or see one of the chaplaincy team in the day centre.

It was about this time that counsellors at Mildmay began to add a really creative edge to their work with parents, children and young people. There was a developing concern to care for the rest of the family as well as the patient. Counsellors now often use puppets to enable younger children to act out family scenes, and materials such as paint and clay are being used to help them express feelings they cannot verbalise. Where appropriate parents are encouraged to compile a 'life book' or collect memorabilia to put into a 'memory box' for their children. The life book may include descriptive pieces written by the parent, letters, poems, photographs, or a family tree, and it can be accompanied by particular items to be given to the child at special times. These might include a dried flower from the mother's wedding bouquet, letters to be opened on the day the child starts school and/or gets married, a piece of jewellery, or a special book. The completed book or box not only creates a beautiful memento for the child, but also offers the parent a chance to express feelings or record special memories. He or she can then feel that at least there will be some ongoing communication with the child, and that family memories will be passed on. I believe this approach has helped many patients achieve a greater peace of mind.

As part of our ongoing care of families, we had set up Remembrance Services, to be held every three or four months. This was something we began early on, and it is still our practice today. Families and friends of the patients who have died in the previous four months are invited to return for a service of remembrance for their loved one, together with many others. During the service the first names of those who have died are read out. Prayers are offered for those recently bereaved, the choir sings, and poems, readings and a short talk are interspersed with some hymns. The service is followed by a time when families and friends can meet together, chatting to staff and each other while they relax with a cup of coffee. Again it is a relief for many of these people to be able to talk openly about their loved one. Many people, whether they are Christian or not, find great comfort in coming to this Christian service. Many come time after time, some even attending every service. We now invite people to bring a flower, or we give them one during the service. In memory of their loved one, they are invited to place the flowers in a piece of oasis contained in a planter. When the floral tributes are formed into a bouquet they are placed in the chapel. People seem to find this gesture very meaningful and helpful as they begin to deal with their bereavement and face life again.

Day nursery

As we observed the increase in the number of women being referred for care, we were also noticing other common features. The average age of the women being admitted at that time was twenty-six years. Most of them were living alone with their babies or small children, with no partner to share the responsibility. Many of the mothers had not known of their HIV status until tested during pregnancy.

If you had asked me then whether I thought it would be a good idea to run a day nursery at Mildmay, my reaction would have been one of surprise. What has that got to do with AIDS palliative care? Which children? Where from? Should they not be in the ordinary nurseries and play schools, not segregated into a specialist service? Why us? I was certainly surprised, and asked just those questions, when we were first approached by Hackney Social Services about the possibility of Mildmay doing just that.

Barnardo's were running a day nursery in Hackney and we were already working with them for the crèche provided once a week during the women's only day in the day centre. As well as offering advice, they had also donated a nursery nurse from their own centre to look after the children every Wednesday. The mothers in the day centre really appreciated this service, because they could relax knowing that their children were nearby and safe. The young children of mothers staying in the wards were also able to use the facility and it proved to be a successful response to the needs of both children and mothers.

Social Services, therefore, already knew that we had the crèche and they were wondering if we could expand the service. We all agreed that to segregate the children of HIV positive mothers may not be ideal, but the social workers explained that there were no nursery places available for these children in generic nurseries in Hackney. We knew there was an increasing number of small children and babies whose parents were HIV positive or had AIDS in East London, and the need of these children had to be addressed. They needed to be treated as individuals, not as mere appendages to either parent.

Social Services had a strong case for asking us to help. With the stigma and prejudice surrounding a diagnosis of AIDS, mothers felt unable to disclose their diagnosis. Had they felt able to do so, their child could have been identified as having 'special needs', but fears about lack of confidentiality were paralysing them. At Mildmay we had been caring for people with AIDS for four years now. We were fully aware of the problems these families were facing, and had firm policies related to confidentiality. We were also in the right area 'geographically' to service these families, and if help with the children were available, families could be supported for longer in the community during episodes of ill health. Importantly, we already had some experience, albeit limited, of caring for these children and such experience was scarce at the time. Not only that, but we had a hall with an adjacent outdoor area which, with only minor refurbishment, could satisfy the strict registration requirements.

Soon after his appointment sometime earlier, we had been visited by Dr Kenneth Calman, the Chief Medical Officer of Health, and Mr Herbert Laming, the Chief Inspector of Social Services. They had been very interested in the work and very supportive. As Mr Laming was leaving he had said, 'If there is ever anything I can do to help, let me know.' That is the kind of comment one does not forget, and I felt that I would now take him up on his offer. I contacted his office and asked if I could arrange to see him personally, even if only for ten minutes. I felt that ten minutes with him would be worth more than two hours with anyone else, and anyway I had something I very much wanted to tell him.

I told him in detail of this growing problem in the East End of London. I explained the problems concerning disclosure of the diagnosis, and said that I was aware of the many competing priorities, within limited resources, with which the social workers were having to cope. Compared to problems of child abuse and homelessness, the problems of these children could not always be seen as a priority. I told him that we had been approached for help. What did he think we should do? If his advice was that it would be inappropriate for us to be involved, I would have to take that advice and other solutions to the problem would have to be found. At least I would have made him aware that the problem existed and was growing, and I felt strongly that he should know about it. If we were to be involved in providing the nursery service, however, we would require £5,000 capital to refurbish and equip the hall, and we would need to ensure that revenue funding would be available for the service.

I was grateful to be given an appointment with this very busy man and we spent an hour together discussing the matter. He was, as I had expected him to be, very interested to gather information about this new situation and obviously saw the need to do something about it. He encouraged us to go ahead, in consultation with social workers, mothers and health care professionals involved locally, setting up a service that would at least provide the best solution to the problem for the time being. He also promised to investigate sources of funding. I thanked him, and as we walked to the lift at the end of my visit, he said with a smile, 'What else could I say?'

The nursery service was duly planned, initially to operate three days a week for a year. During that year the Social Services would invest resources in training childminders and foster parents locally to care for these children at home. All the monies needed for the first year were provided, the revenue by North East Thames Regional Health Authority and the capital by the Department of Social Services, and the aim was to open the nursery as soon as possible.

Growing responsibilities

The organisation at Mildmay was growing rapidly and staff numbers had quadrupled in the last five years. As this growth took place, and the widespread NHS reforms began to be implemented, changes were necessary within Mildmay if we were to be successful in the new 'contract culture'. We wanted Mildmay to be a leader and not a follower.

Mildmay's expertise in the field of AIDS palliative medicine was now well recognised and medical consultancy requests were increasing. Patients were voting with their feet and were asking to come to Mildmay for their care. There were four full-time doctors by now, and they provided continuity of care for the patients by covering for the whole twenty-four hours rather than using locums, who would not know the patients.

The necessity to concentrate on the increasing medical responsibility meant that the Medical Director could no longer lead the planning and development side of things as well. The Board of Directors therefore decided to appoint me as Chief Executive of Mildmay with overall responsibility for the organisation, including strategic planning and developments. I would need further training if I was to be effective in this new role, and so explored the possibilities with the Board's support.

The programme that I identified as being the one that would best fit my own and Mildmay's needs was the Top Managers' Programme at Kings' Fund College. I was familiar with their learning environment and style as I had been part of their Senior Managers' Development Programme three years before. The TMP also had an emphasis on management development and the programme lasted for one year. It was clearly NHS focused, but I felt I needed to understand the working of the reformed health service better if Mildmay was to compete successfully for contracts. Another bonus would be the networking opportunities to be had when working with other chief executives of purchaser and provider units. The main problem was that it was very expensive, as all such courses are. Where was I going to be able to find over £6,000 to fund this training? Mildmay could certainly not afford to pay that much.

I decided to approach the Department of Health to see if they would sponsor me to do the course. AIDS money was still ringfenced at that time and I felt that the training of managers for AIDS services, which were expanding in response to increased demand, had to be seen as a priority. Fortunately they agreed. I was sponsored on the understanding that after the course I would stay at Mildmay for a reasonable time so that it would benefit from the training opportunity I had been given. It has always been my experience that if God gives you a job to do He always equips you to do it. Here was more evidence to support that belief!

Mark's story

There were so many palpable achievements to celebrate during this centenary year. But the patients were the priority and we were also celebrating successes with them and their families. Mark's was one such success story and sums up so well what Mildmay could offer.

Mark had been living with his parents. He got on well with his mother, but not so well with his father, who had never come to terms with the fact that Mark was gay. He was ashamed and refused to talk about it. Mark came with his mother to 'have a look round' before deciding whether he wanted to be admitted to Mildmay or not. He had been referred for terminal care and ideally would have liked to stay at home. His parents worked, however, and he was too frightened to spend all day alone.

I remember meeting Mark in reception. In his early twenties, he looked very smart in a suit as he made his way to the desk with the support of two sticks. He told me later that he and his mother had gone out and bought the suit and new shoes especially for his visit to Mildmay. Having looked around and met the staff, he decided he would come in and was admitted the next day. He was suffering from peripheral neuropathy, causing pain in his feet, and a widespread atypical tuberculosis. He had been ill on and off for over two years with many admissions to hospital.

Within twenty-four hours of admission Mark developed acute abdominal pain and the team felt that he should return to his acute hospital for investigations and possible surgery. He was seen by the doctor and his primary nurse, who discussed the possible options and likely outcomes with him. He asked if he could have two hours to decide and requested a visit from the local Roman Catholic parish priest (a man not known to him). He talked with the priest and was given the last rites. At 4.00 p.m. he told the team he had decided that he did not wish to go back to hospital for any more treatment. He knew that he might die quite soon, but that was his choice and he told his mother of his decision. Over a period of a few hours, it seemed, this boy had become a man. In fact, Mark did not die suddenly. He lived for another year as the result of treatment prescribed primarily for the control of symptoms.

At first his father would not visit him, but after a couple of days he did and the nurses noticed that he only stayed for a few minutes. If anyone approached him he would leave immediately. As time went by, however, both he and his wife began to spend longer with Mark and the team, especially the counsellor and chaplain, were able to support them. Mark's condition stabilised and for a time he actually improved a great deal. This time was very important to him and his parents. It was a time during which they could work through painful issues, with the help of the counsellor and the rest of the team, and they emerged with an openness and honesty that, as a family, they had never known before.

Mark never gave up his wish to die at home. His mother felt guilty that she was out at work and unable to cope with caring for him. In the end Mark decided he would like to go home for the odd day at the weekend. This was carefully arranged so that the whole family felt supported and had adequate back-up.

Later on Mark developed CMV retinitis. He had dreaded this because, apart from the possibility of becoming blind, he really was needle phobic and the treatment usually involved injections or the insertion of a permanent central line. Again he spent a day or so thinking about his options and decided he could not risk going blind. He would therefore have to have the treatment and returned to his acute centre to have a Hickman Line sited. His infusions would be given through this permanently inserted intravenous line, which meant that he did not need to have daily injections.

By now his mother was more confident about Mark's visits home, his relationship with his father was much better and he really wanted to spend more time at home. But what about the infusions? His parents felt quite unable to take this on and he could still only go home for the odd day. Community care for a Hickman Line was not available at that time.

As his condition deteriorated, Mark took control of the situation. As he still wanted to be at home when he died, he decided that he would learn how to infuse the medication through the Hickman Line himself. He felt very strongly that he needed the freedom to control his environment rather than having the environment control him. His mother was also taught how to give the infusion and gradually they both became more confident. She had decided by now to give up her job so that she could care for Mark at home. The home care nurses visited Mark and his family in Mildmay and he was glad to establish relationships that would continue when he went home.

His discharge was carefully planned so that he had several trial weekends before finally going home. He regularly contacted the ward to let the team know how he was, and his mother cared for him with only the minimum of input needed from community services. This was as Mark wanted it. After twelve weeks he died peacefully at home, his parents well supported by the home care team and the priest who was now their friend.

Mark did manage to take control of his life. He was allowed to make choices for himself, with outcomes that his family and the staff sometimes found difficult and challenging. During the last few months of his illness, however, he achieved an enormous amount. He overcame tremendous personal fears and obstacles to make his wish to die at home become a reality.

Giving control to the patients, where it belongs, is often easier said than done. It involves accepting a challenge and having the courage to change things. It means being innovative, working out new ways of solving problems, taking risks and being willing to accept difficult outcomes. But above all, it means reinforcing the value that we as carers place on those for whom we care – those people who, with courage and dignity, are taking control of their situation and who are allowing us the privilege of sharing their lives. This was what we set out to do at Mildmay, and our success in doing it was certainly something we could celebrate in our centenary year.

9
A TIME OF THANKSGIVING
1992

Centenary Service

The procession of some sixty robed clergy heralded the start
and finish of a memorable and special evening for Mildmay. It
was 4th November, and we were at St Paul's Cathedral for a
grand Thanksgiving Service. Dr George Carey, the Archbishop
of Canterbury, said it was an enormous pleasure for him to be
able to join in Mildmay's centenary celebrations by giving the
sermon at the service. His association with Mildmay was
perhaps doubly appreciated because he is himself an East End
Londoner, born and bred. The service celebrated a hundred
years of Christian caring at Mildmay with a harmonious
arrangement of hymns, choir recitals, prayers and scripture
readings. In his sermon, invoking the parable of the Good
Samaritan, Dr Carey called on the thousand-strong audience,
'to look upon people with AIDS as our neighbours and to love
them unconditionally. It is unchristian to believe that AIDS is
God's judgment on them, for God's love is totally indiscrimi-
nate.' Dr Carey maintained that Mildmay had been a neighbour
and friend to countless people in need, and that its history
imitated the actions of the Good Samaritan himself.

The clergy who attended represented the myriad arms of the
Christian Church, ranging from the Church of England and the
Roman Catholic Church to the Free Church, including the
Salvation Army, and internationally the French Protestant,
Dutch Reformed and Greek Orthodox Churches. The congre-
gation meanwhile comprised staff and supporters from all walks
of life. We considered it a great privilege to be able to welcome

the many individuals to St Paul's and to share with them in a time of thanksgiving. This was to be the first of our Annual Thanksgiving Services, which now form part of the Christian life of the hospital, together with our regular services of remembrance for the families and friends of the patients who have died at Mildmay. A Mildmay staff choir was formed to sing at all these services and other special events.

A private reception in the crypt of St Paul's followed the centenary Thanksgiving Service and enabled us to give a more personal show of appreciation to some of our major supporters over the years. Dr Carey had become acquainted with Mildmay's work through his visit to us in 1991 soon after he became Archbishop of Canterbury. He referred to his special association with Mildmay in an article he wrote for the *Mail on Sunday*, headlined, 'The Hope that will forever light the gloom'. In the article he described how the spiritual component of care at Mildmay had illuminated the life of one young girl in the AIDS unit.

A well-known visitor

Just a few days after our Thanksgiving Service, there was more excitement. Elizabeth Taylor, international film star and leading AIDS campaigner in the United States, made a morale-boosting visit to Mildmay on 7th November. At her own request this was essentially a private visit and therefore the flashing cameras of the paparazzi normally in attendance were conspicuously absent. This was a calculated effort on her behalf to focus attention on meeting patients and staff, rather than creating a blaze of publicity for herself. The genuineness of the gesture was warmly appreciated.

For one and a half hours the then newly-married Mrs Fortensky easily switched between light-hearted chatter and serious conversation in both the residential unit and the day centre, talking for long periods to patients in the privacy of their own rooms. Of special interest to her were Mildmay's plans for the expansion of the AIDS care programme in our centenary year, including the planned unit for mothers and children.

Some nurses and patients asked for her postcards and assorted memorabilia to be autographed, and artist Kevin, from the day centre, was delighted that she accepted one of his watercolours with enthusiasm.

Special memories

That centenary year was certainly full of remarkable events, and it was also memorable for some special characters among the patients at Mildmay. Let me share just a few of their stories.

This year the Carol Service was special. It was the first time a patient had chosen to take an active part in a major service. David's insistence on coming to the service was matched only by his defiance of the pain of his disability. While free from pain most of the time, he certainly experienced discomfort when sitting in his wheelchair. Nonetheless, he managed the most precise of emphases throughout an exceptionally eloquent Bible reading of the passage from Isaiah chapter 9 beginning 'Unto us a child is born'. Having celebrated Christmas and seen in the New Year, he died with us shortly after.

Another patient who lived and died with us was Jonathan. I had heard that he was depressed and, when I met him, I was not surprised about this. He was only in his late twenties and was suffering from Kaposi's sarcoma, a form of skin cancer which in his case had resulted in purple lesions all over his body. Not only was the Kaposi's sarcoma affecting his skin, but he had it internally too and his lymph glands were affected. This had resulted in oedema (swelling) of his limbs and most other parts of his body. He had one large lesion at the end of his nose and various others on his face. His face was swollen and in the morning when he woke up he was unable to open his eyes until he had been sitting up for some time. His hair was thin and sparse although he was only a young man. His arms, hands, legs and feet were all swollen and puffy, and as the day went on he would have great difficulty in walking.

Jonathan had been a very handsome young man and to have his youthful good looks replaced by the disfigurement he was experiencing must have been very hard. I first met him towards the end of his life, when he was feeling extremely depressed and weary. By that time the skin on his legs had broken and was leaking and ulcerating in places from his groin to his toes. As I had specialised in the care of people with malignant wounds before coming to Mildmay, I had been asked to visit him to advise on the care of his legs.

I was shown into his room and, although the legs were kept clean, because of the constant discharge the unpleasant smell was the first thing I encountered. Jonathan was sitting on a special cushion in a recliner chair with his legs raised and covered with a sterile towel. As I looked at him I felt a deep sadness. My previous work with patients with malignant wounds had helped me to understand how they felt about living with profound disfigurement and wounds that would not heal. They could never forget about it. It was always there – the discomfort, the discharge and the odour. As I greeted him he did not smile, but looked at me through swollen eyelids and said, 'You will never have seen anything like this, it's horrible. You won't be able to do anything for me, will you?'

I washed my hands, opened the dressing pack and removed the sheet from his legs. 'Sometimes Lord,' I thought to myself, 'I can't understand how this can be allowed to happen to anyone, but I know I only see part of the picture. I can't confess to understand. This beautiful young man is being destroyed by this virus in the prime of his life. Look at his hair, his eyes, his nose – just like a clown, but it's not funny. Fine movements of his hands are lost to him, and now these legs, weeping, ulcerated, uncomfortable and terrible to look at – especially if they are your legs.' I kept these thoughts to myself, however.

I told Jonathan I could help him and I would like to suggest a different treatment. He said, 'Will it really improve things? I know I haven't got long left, but if we can dry up this discharge a bit and deal with the smell, I'll feel better about myself.'

Following consultation with the interdisciplinary team, treatment was started and two days later I visited Jonathan again. It was lunchtime and he was sitting up in his chair. As I knocked and walked in, he greeted me: 'Much better already. Now they don't smell so much, I feel a bit less embarrassed.'

A few days later, however, he asked to see Veronica, our Medical Director. He told her that he had had enough. 'Look at me, you shouldn't treat a dog like this. I don't want to be kept alive. I want to ask if you could please end it all for me? I'm going to die anyway, and the longer I live the worse I'm going to get. Can't you take pity on me?'

Veronica explained to him that as a doctor and also a Christian she could not help him in that way. She agreed with him that his quality of life was poor, but she pointed out that he need not suffer physical pain and she would do all that she could to keep him comfortable and try to alleviate his distress.

They continued to talk and in the course of their conversation she said to him, 'Do you believe in God?'

'Yes I do,' he said, 'but I keep talking to Him and asking Him to take me home. But He's not really doing much for me, is He?'

Veronica asked him if he would like them to pray together. He said he would. Jonathan prayed first, saying, 'Dear God, look at me, what a mess I'm in and you know I want to come home to you as soon as possible. Please take me home.'

When he had finished, Veronica prayed and asked God to comfort and be with Jonathan at that time. She asked Jonathan if he would like to see Peter, the Senior Chaplain. Although he had previously refused, now he felt that he would like to. During the next few days Peter spent a lot of time with Jonathan, who organised his own funeral service and arranged to have joyful hymns. He finished what he called 'unfinished business'. He wrote to some friends and telephoned others and gradually, as his condition deteriorated, it was noticeable that his extreme unhappiness and agitation had been overtaken by a real sense of peace.

He died ten days after speaking to Veronica. He did not die alone. Peter was with him and said the Lord's Prayer and, as he said 'Amen', Jonathan squeezed his hand. A few moments later he died peacefully.

Michael was another of our patients I particularly remember from that year. He was loved by patients and staff alike, a very special person and full of courage. It was remarkable how he was always so cheerful and ready with a kind word or helpful action for any of the other patients.

Michael also had Kaposi's sarcoma, and he had it so badly over his face and head that the colour of his skin looked almost deep mauve. Although he had slight oedema of his legs, it was not as bad as Jonathan and, until the last few days of his life, he could still walk. His upper limbs were not affected and in Michael's case this was a real blessing.

Since the beginning of his illness and disfigurement Michael had spent time talking to nurses and doctors about how he felt about his condition and teaching them about Kaposi's sarcoma. I went to visit him one morning and was made very welcome. 'Come in and sit down. I like having people to talk to and I want to show you something,' he said to me. 'You know I have been in Mildmay several times over this past year, and while I've been here I've been making use of my time.'

I told him that I heard he was popular with the other patients and with a smile he said, 'I keep them occupied, you see, we've been busy. Did you know that I make tapestries? I've been doing it for years. It's been more difficult more recently. My fine movements are not what they were, but I have managed to finish what I've been making here. Look in that cupboard over there, please, and fetch me that large blue bag.'

I went to the cupboard, found the bag and brought it to Michael. 'Open it,' he said. I opened the bag and brought out the most beautiful tapestry. 'Those colours have been specially chosen to match the chapel, as I've made the tapestry to be hung there. Look at the back first.' I looked, and at the back I saw a mass of neat but loose threads, with no semblance of a pattern. 'Now turn it over,' he said. On the other side, the chaos was transformed into beauty. It was a picture of doves in a peaceful garden.

Michael said, 'This tapestry is special because there is a hidden meaning in it. It speaks of life and of people who have lived here at Mildmay, because every patient I have met here, in my in-patient stays, in the day centre, and on the wards has contributed to the creation of this beautiful tapestry. Together we have created something for Mildmay, something that the patients who follow after us, and their families and friends and anybody who uses the chapel, will be able to share. They won't know about the hidden meaning, but the staff here now do, and they will pass it on and we won't be forgotten.'

I thanked Michael for the beautiful gift and realised how creative God had been with this young man despite all his pain and discomfort, both emotional and physical. He had been able to create something himself, something of beauty, and through this had been able to realise his own value and to encourage other patients to see that they all had a contribution to make, however small. I thought of his disfigured face and his courage and his smile. I believe God's healing for Michael had come through his being enabled to live, really live, until he died.

The tapestry now hangs in our chapel and we never see it without remembering Michael and thanking God for him. Peter, our Senior Chaplain, said of the tapestry: 'This gift will always remind me of the two ways of looking at life, and how a work of art should not be judged by one side alone. Whereas from an earthly point of view we often see the back of life, ("We see through a glass – darkly", from 1 Cor 13:12 AV), God sees it from the front, the side of truth, beauty, meaning and a clear message of love.'

I have often said that we are so privileged to be involved with our patients at this special time in their lives, and if we have learned anything then it is they who have been our teachers.

Training trainers in East Africa

Learning from many different sources, of course, was going on all the time, and we were involved in an expanding programme of more formal training. The most exciting part of that, perhaps, was the development of plans triggered off by our visit to Africa in 1991.

To be a person with AIDS in many areas of Kenya at the moment is a frightening and hopeless situation to be in if you are poor and have little family support. You are unlikely to be seen by a doctor and won't be able to pay for the drugs if you do. Surgery? X-ray? Chemotherapy? Radiotherapy? Can't afford it. And you'll need to keep your diagnosis a secret if you don't want to become isolated. As you become weaker you'll find it increasingly difficult to find the money to support yourself and if you are admitted to hospital, you will probably be sent home to die.

Thus ran my report for the Smith & Nephew Foundation/ Florence Nightingale Scholarship which had funded my trip to Kenya, Uganda and Zimbabwe.

Having designed in outline our first international Training of Trainers course and having received approval for it from the ODA, we were ready to conduct the first course in Kenya. In order to ensure that the programme would be culturally sensitive, we had met in London with one of the Kenyan facilitators, Esther Gatua, who would work with us on the programme. We had gone through the programme in detail together and she had advised us on the content for each session. We then arranged to meet her in Kenya two days before the course commenced to finalise the programme.

The participants consisted of senior health care professionals, doctors, nurses, counsellors and social workers. We were there to facilitate their training on the care, management and counselling of people with AIDS and their families. Part of the work was also for them to develop their own projects or training programmes and exciting proposals were the result. One such project was the establishment of a day centre in a large room at one of the local hospitals. The opening of this was to coincide with the days when the AIDS outpatient clinics took place. Another important facet of the course was to develop the training and presentational skills of the participants. The provision of supporting hand-out material for each session proved to be invaluable in a country where written material is scarce. The course was thoroughly evaluated and deemed a success. In consequence we were invited to conduct this same basic programme in Uganda and Tanzania in the following years. It was wonderfully encouraging to see such opportunities opening up for Mildmay to share its expertise.

As well as going to Africa to conduct in-country training programmes, we were also providing training at Mildmay for people from all over the world. Many attended courses and seminars held at Mildmay and joined the work placement programmes which were held every month. The demand for places on these placement programmes became so great that at one point in 1992 we had a waiting list of about eighteen months. The benefit of our international placements was not only for the participants, but also for Mildmay in that we learned a great deal about the AIDS scene in other countries and about how they were responding to the problem.

We wanted to formalise our growing international training activities in some way, and on World AIDS Day in 1992 we launched Mildmay's International AIDS Programme (MIAP). To celebrate the launch we held a lunch in Buxton Hall to which we invited Dr Kenneth Calman, the Chief Medical Officer, and other members of the team from the Department of Health.

Baroness Cumberlege, Parliamentary Undersecretary of State for Health, said in a message to us that we had put the 'world' into World AIDS Day by giving the global treatment to the year's theme of 'A Community Commitment'. She continued, 'AIDS represents the biggest health challenge this century. It is too simplistic to say that, because a massive heterosexual epidemic has not happened in this country, it cannot happen. The potential threat of an epidemic remains, you only need to look at other parts of the world – at Africa, at India. Hardly surprising, therefore, that Africa is to become the focus for Mildmay's international response. Training programmes which encourage self-reliance, self-care, family support, counselling/listening skills and basic care of the sick are essential if Africa is to cope with the thousands of people who are dying now, and the millions more who will die in the next decade.'

The closing comments at the launch were presented by Dr
Calman. He referred to the important contribution that Mildmay had made to the East End of London through its community care over the years, and congratulated the team for
showing that their international AIDS programme was extend-
ing community care into many countries across the world.

Family care

As well as burgeoning training opportunities, the improvements
in facilities for our patients were also developing apace. In our
plans for the new family unit, we had explored the possibility
of refurbishing the old operating suite within the old hospital.
We now realised that the site being considered would only
accommodate five families, and was too small, too cramped and
could not provide us with a cost-effective facility.

Our focus then turned to Sir Graham Rowlandson House, an
existing nurses' home adjacent to the main hospital building
which was no longer being used by the nurses. It was a relatively
new building, having been built in 1976. The proposal was to
demolish this building and erect a new, purpose-built Family
Care Centre in its place.

Mildmay was leased from the Regional Health Authority and
it was therefore necessary to obtain permission from both the
Regional and District Health Authorities. First the plans were
drawn up in consultation with women's groups and carers. One
mother with AIDS, reflecting a view shared by many, said, 'I'm
glad Mildmay has asked us for suggestions and ideas to help
them plan the new unit. It will be easier to stay somewhere
which has been designed with our real needs in mind.' The
plans were duly sent for approval to the Regional Health
Authority who approved them quickly, but approval from the
District Health Authority took longer to come through. This
caused considerable delay, and demolition and building work
could not commence as planned in September 1992. By the end
of the year, however, permission had been given and the revised
plan was to start demolition in the New Year.

Day care developments

Now that the old operating suite had been rejected for use as the family unit, we had other ideas for putting it to good use again. It was becoming increasingly urgent for us to find a better site for the day care centre. It had been operating at the open end of Alexandra Ward, but growing problems had been experienced with the mixing of in- and out-patients. When the day patients left every afternoon, the residents on Alexandra Ward would enjoy the facility and were disappointed or even resentful that they could not use it during weekdays, feeling that 'their space' was being invaded. Day patients, on the other hand, were being made to feel that they were intruding on residential patients' territory. It even reached the stage where sauce bottles were individually labelled in the shared kitchen!

The way Alexandra Ward was set out did not help the situation. It is on the second floor of the hospital and is reached either by stairs or a lift. As you entered the ward, at that time, the eight single room units for residential patients were to the left and to the right was the large open area that was the day centre during the day. At the end of the ward was the residential patients' day room, which could only be reached by going through the day centre area.

Having the day centre on the second floor made access difficult, for a start. People in wheelchairs could not find their way easily and independently from the front entrance of Mildmay to the day centre. When the new, easily operated lift was installed, this became less of a problem, but the situation was not ideal.

The most significant problem, however, was rooted in the different stages of illness of the two groups. Although some of the day patients were very sick, there were few who were in the terminal stage of the illness. They tended to be able to look after themselves still, although they had intermittent illnesses and infections. On the other hand, the patients on the ward included those who had been admitted for terminal or long-term care. These patients were encouraged to take part in the life of the ward for as long as possible, and many of them would be seen spending time in the day room or moving from place to place. The problem went both ways. Some residential patients said they felt almost on show to day patients whom they did not know. One young man, however, could be found in the daytime lying on the settee in the day room until the day he died. The day patients found this difficult to cope with. They said it was like a constant reminder that they had an illness and it aroused in them fears for their own future: 'Will I become like that?'

These problems were real and only too understandable. The day care centre had to be resited, and the still-redundant old operating theatre seemed the ideal solution.

We made a bid to the Regional Health Authority for funding to refurbish the theatre suite and were successful in obtaining the money. Most of the transformation was handled by Mildmay's maintenance team. The refurbishment work was extensive, including electrical rewiring, fire alarm installation, painting, plumbing and fabric modification. The equipment stripped out from the theatre was given to ECHO, an organisation that supplied refurbished equipment to developing countries. Nothing was ever wasted during our refurbishments!

The new facilities for day care included a large lounge and kitchen, counselling room, a massage or examination room, a craft activity area and a staff office. A wide range of services from the interdisciplinary team was available to day care patients. The centre was intended for anyone with a diagnosis of AIDS or symptomatic HIV disease. It was not a drop-in centre: attendance was by prior arrangement with the centre staff. It also afforded clients the opportunity for social interaction with others who had similar problems, and they had their own organised programme of events, including parties and outings.

The provision of day care was important as part of the overall services at Mildmay, but it did not work quite as I had expected it to. When I had been in San Francisco I had seen day care being used for two main purposes. The first was the administration of intravenous therapies and treatments, and the second was as respite for carers who needed to go to work. In the latter case, patients would be brought to the centre at about 8.00 a.m. and picked up at the end of the day. Although we had planned to provide for the same sort of care our centre did not function in the same way.

As more and more patients were being taught how to give their own intravenous therapies at home, there was no longer a need for them to come to us. We did provide this service for the occasional patient and also enabled some to have their inhaled pentamidine with us (a treatment given to prevent a form of pneumonia common in people with AIDS), but those people were few in number. Our clients were also in greater need of respite and general care for themselves, rather than respite for their carers. Most of our patients lived alone and did not have carers, and it was interesting to note the differences between the needs of those coming to Mildmay and the patients I had seen in the States. One of our patients' greatest needs was for the social interaction that the day centre would provide. They were coming to Mildmay to have a good time, to meet other people, to have a nourishing meal and to avail themselves of the treatment and advice on offer from the interdisciplinary team.

Home care changes

When the day centre moved, the original home care service was also restructured. The home care team had been set up primarily to provide care for people in their own homes and to enable those who wished to do so to remain at home for terminal care and to die there. In order to provide a high quality service we had appointed a team of senior nursing staff. They were all registered nurses who had district nursing certificates and who, if they did not have it already, would undertake the ENB 934 Course (the Care and Management of people with AIDS and their families) during the first year of their appointment.

Part of their role was to provide advice on symptom control and care of people with AIDS to primary care teams, i.e. GPs, district nurses and health visitors, among others. For this part of their work there was constant demand. They liaised with primary health care teams and social services staff, and made new contacts to the benefit of the patients. As far as care of patients in their own homes was concerned, however, the nurses felt they were becoming deskilled. They were visiting patients to check that they were all right, but found that in the majority of cases, as soon as someone became ill (and this could happen very suddenly for a person with AIDS), he or she wanted to 'go in somewhere', usually the acute hospital but sometimes for palliative care service.

In my previous experience it had proved very difficult to provide twenty-four-hour care in the community for highly dependent patients, irrespective of their diagnosis, and it was certainly no different in the case of these patients. I remember one young man who was desperate to die at home. He had no family or friends to care for him and, in order to provide the twenty-four-hour cover he needed, twenty-two different agencies were involved. Having said that, to this day I am still not sure whether patients are, or are not, choosing to die at home. Perhaps they have no choice at all because the services are not available, or perhaps fear, anxiety and other distressing symptoms result in their request for admission. I do know that for patients on their own, or for their families looking on, symptoms such as difficulty in breathing, profuse diarrhoea and mental health problems as a result of HIV dementia can be frightening and difficult to cope with. Many of our patients lose consciousness several days before they die and some carers do not feel able to care for an unconscious patient at home.

In San Francisco it seemed that many more people with AIDS did die at home with family and a circle of friends organising a rota of care. One factor may have been that people with AIDS there could have funding for a care assistant for four hours a day once they had an AIDS diagnosis, and for eight hours a day during the last ten days of their lives. Many of our patients in London just do not seem to have the same opportunities. Many are separated from their families and appear not to have friends who are in a position to care for them at home. This being the case, I feel strongly that we at Mildmay have a privilege in becoming close to, and sharing the lives of, these lonely people who are facing loss of independence and, ultimately, death.

With all these factors in mind, the home care team was disbanded in its original form in 1992 and restructured to form a Community Liaison Service. The purpose of this service was to assist with continuity of care for patients moving from the community into hospital or hospice and back to the community. It was hoped that the reorganisation would more effectively respond to the changing needs of our patients and clients. This new service also involved continuing contact with patients in their own homes and the provision of specialist knowledge and clinical skills to GPs, district nurses and other home carers. The team would also be involved in liaison with and co-ordination of various agencies to provide care and support to the patient, his or her family and significant others in the community. A major aspect of their work was to take referrals for admission to Mildmay, to ensure smooth admissions and discharges, and to act as consultants to hospice and community nurses and other agencies.

Achievements so far

Mildmay's centenary year had seen some major changes and developments in our work. It had been a packed year, but at the end of it we could certainly look back and give thanks to God for what had been achieved, both in that year and since the AIDS work had begun.

One hundred years on and four years after starting our AIDS work, our position at the end of 1992 looked like this:

- Helen Ward had opened and we now had three wards
- Our debts were paid and Mildmay had financial stability
- Our international work had been launched
- Plans for a family care centre had been prepared and approved
- The day centre had been refurbished and moved

● The home care nurses had become the Community Liaison
  Team, with a wider remit

Now firmly established and internationally respected for our
work, we could continue in confidence to broaden the scope of
our provision for the growing number of AIDS patients. More
challenges lay ahead, of that we were sure.

10

A TIME TO PULL DOWN AND
A TIME TO BUILD
1993

The building of the Family Care Centre

With the excitements of the centenary year behind us, it was time to concentrate on the long-awaited Family Care Centre. The two years following 1992 saw thrilling developments for Mildmay in Africa also, but the Family Centre deserves a chapter of its own.

By early 1993 we had the site and the plans, the estimated capital costs being £3.3 million. An Appeal Committee had been set up, but the country was in economic recession and we were aware of an increasing number of charities who were being forced to close because of lack of donations. We had the necessary official approvals, but we only had a quarter of a million pounds in the Family Care Centre account.

One thing we did have in abundance was faith, and this faith was helped by the fact that we had seen God provide for Mildmay's needs through the years. We believed that He wanted us to expand and build this Centre, and so we planned to go ahead. The Appeal Committee was made up of many people, including some Christian businessmen working in the City. When they heard that we were to start a £3.3 million project with only a quarter of a million in the bank, some resigned from the Appeal Committee and one of them wrote to the Board, stating that Mildmay was heading for bankruptcy. Despite that, the Board endorsed the decision to commence work and in January, Sir Graham Rowlandson House was demolished. We had set a target to open the first beds to patients nine months later, in September, and so weekly meetings were held with the

Project Manager, Design Team and Building Contractor, to ensure that the programme stayed on target. Some of the staff have since referred to my 'cracking the whip' in order to keep things going, and perhaps I did!

The foundations were in place by 24th March, when the foundation stone was laid by Baroness Cumberlege, Parliamentary Undersecretary for Health. She applauded Mildmay for its century of care, love and compassion. 'The thing that I love about Mildmay,' she said, 'is that it is all the time moving forward, seeing gaps, meeting new needs. Mildmay has recognised the difficulties that parents face when they are ill and have nobody to care for their children and, of course, with HIV/AIDS there may well be the added complication that both parent and child are ill at the same time. I know that they will provide in this new facility the same caring and high quality services that has characterised their work in this field.' To resounding applause, the Baroness was then presented with a posy of flowers by Dean, the eighteen-month-old son of Billy and Iola, who had AIDS. (Dean was later the first child to be baptised in Mildmay's chapel, a happy ceremony that we all shared.)

The foundation stone ceremony was concluded by Peter Clarke, our Senior Chaplain, who offered a prayer of dedication for the new centre. He referred to Jesus as 'Our Master Builder, the Great Healer and the Foundation of our Faith.' He thanked God for bestowing on humanity the gifts of imagination and creative skills which enabled pioneering projects such as the Family Care Centre to be achieved. Quoting from Psalm 127 verse 1, he declared, 'Unless the Lord builds the House, those who build it labour in vain' (RSV). God had given us the confidence to go ahead with the building of this Centre and with His blessing the building had taken shape.

The residential accommodation was arranged on three floors, and included the following facilities:

● twelve large family rooms for mother or father and child, each with balcony and en suite bathroom

- interlinking rooms to accommodate families when more than one member is ill
- separate suites to allow other loved ones not requiring medical care to stay close by
- day care nursery for up to twenty children (doubling the capacity of the previous facilities in Buxton Hall)
- therapy and counselling rooms
- lounge and dining room areas
- enclosed gardens and conservatory
- additional (assisted) bathrooms
- kitchen and laundry facilities

The finishes and interiors of the Family Care Centre had been as carefully designed as the exterior. The architect had advised us on colours, furniture and fabrics and the outcome was something very beautiful which is enjoyed by visitors and patients alike. Apart from the nursery, which is the most beautiful I have ever seen and where primary colours are in evidence everywhere, the colours are gentle and mellow, giving the centre an aura of peace and tranquillity.

The topping out ceremony, which took place when the building was almost completed, traditionally involves the laying of the final brick. I was asked to lay it and had to be raised on a crane to the topmost level of the building. As I am terrified of heights, this caused me some anxiety and the rest of the staff a great deal of amusement! I looked about and saw such a different scene from the foundation stone ceremony just six months previously. The building's steel frame, which had stood bare and stark in January, had been transformed by the cladding of several thousand yellow bricks.

A week before the centre was due to open for patients, an open week was held according to our usual practice. Various groups of people, including health care professionals, purchasers, planners of services, architects and VIPs from the Department of Health and Houses of Commons and Lords, were invited on different days. On the media day there was an enormous response. Television crews and the national press were in attendance, but so many came from the international press that we had to hold a special session for them. It was good to think that information about Mildmay's work, especially with families, was going to be news in many parts of the world.

After a hectic building schedule spanning just eight months, Mildmay's Family Care Centre – the first of its kind in the world – opened its doors to patients on 21st September 1993, amid joyous celebration and grateful relief. It seemed somehow fitting that, at an International Conference in Edinburgh that same year, Dr Michael Merson, Executive Director of the World Health Organisation's Global Programme on AIDS, should make the following comment: 'A decade ago women and children seemed to be on the periphery of the AIDS epidemic. Today women and children are at the centre of our concern. AIDS has not spared them . . . but, though there is no cure yet for HIV infection or AIDS, people's suffering and isolation can be lessened by appropriate treatment, support and care.'

Princess Diana opens the Family Centre

We were so delighted when the Princess of Wales honoured our long-standing invitation to conduct the official opening of Mildmay's Family Care Centre on 21st September 1993. The essentially private visit had to remain a closely guarded secret in view of the immense publicity surrounding her decision to retire temporarily from public life. Free from the glare of press photo calls, the two-hour morning visit proved a relaxed and informative occasion.

After having performed the official task of cutting the ribbon in the reception area, the Princess made her way to the first stop, the Family Care Centre's nursery. There were excited screams and squeals as the older children recognised their special visitor. The little ones investigated somewhat more cautiously in the reassuring presence of their nursery nurse. Surrounded by a medley of books, equipment, toys and several adoring children, the Princess was invited to have a pretend cup of tea, play some games and indulge in a spot of juggling. She was highly amused at the children's antics, teasing them and ruffling their hair, much to their vocal delight. She even tried on a fireman's helmet.

Fun and games it may well have been for most of the children, but the high spirits in the playroom are a far cry from the underlying seriousness of the patient care delivered to the fathers and mothers whom the Princess met next on the floors above. She spent over forty minutes listening to their personal stories and sharing with them. I have accompanied many visitors, but the Princess certainly showed a greater understanding of the patients' emotional needs than most. One woman said that the ability to open up so honestly about her fears and concerns to the Princess, who encouraged, consoled and displayed such genuine interest, had contributed to this being the best day of her life. This was Princess Diana's third visit and every time I met her my respect for her increased. The fact that she had come despite having a very nasty cold, which would have kept most people indoors, was further evidence to me of how genuinely she cared about Mildmay.

After having viewed the rest of the centre's facilities we were able to brief the Princess on Mildmay's International AIDS Programme and the strong links being developed between Mildmay and Africa. She asked us to keep her informed. She then met staff informally over drinks and allowed both staff and patients to take photographs. It was a wonderful visit and it meant so much to us that she had come yet again, this time despite the fact that she was simultaneously having to deal with so many personal issues.

It was the last time that Mrs Taylor Thompson was to meet Princess Diana as Chairman of Mildmay. She was shortly to retire as Chairman and take on the responsibility of President. She and Lord McColl, the President, were in fact going to exchange roles and he would therefore become Mildmay's new Chairman. Mrs Helen Taylor Thompson had no plans, however, to step back from her work for Mildmay. She was already working for the Friends of Mildmay, and was also intending to be involved in fundraising for Mildmay's International AIDS Programme.

Now that the Family Centre was up and running, we soon saw the benefits. We were so pleased to have the facilities which enabled us to meet the needs of these precious families. The best way to illustrate this is to tell you about some of the families we were able to help through the centre.

Cathy and Eddie

Cathy is now twenty-four years old, a blue-eyed blonde, and has been married to Eddie since she was seventeen years old. Eddie is now thirty years old, a handsome young Irishman with brown hair and blue eyes. They have two children – Mary, aged two, and Rosie, aged five. Cathy and Eddie were brought up in Ireland and became intravenous drug users in their teens. They moved to London and for two years had successfully been off drugs.

When Cathy became pregnant with Mary, however, she was tested and found to be HIV positive. Eddie and Rosie were then also tested and Eddie was found to be positive, but to everyone's relief, Rosie was negative. The stress of all this resulted in their return to drugs and a chaotic lifestyle. Cathy and Eddie have a stormy relationship, but emotionally they are very dependent on each other. They live together with their children in a one-bedroomed flat in East London. They do not get on with their neighbours, who they say are hostile to them. Eddie is frequently in trouble with the police due to repeated thefts in order to finance their illegal drug use. He has been in prison on several occasions.

For the last year, Cathy and Eddie have both had frequent illnesses. Cathy's parents, who live in Ireland, have tried to be very supportive to the family. They have had the children to stay when Cathy and Eddie have both been ill, but when this has not been possible the children have had to be taken into care urgently, with temporary foster parents. This has proved to be unsatisfactory, as the children fretted and Rosie started wetting the bed again.

Cathy and Eddie were both diagnosed last year as having

AIDS, and have had increasingly frequent admissions to hospital and to Mildmay. The baby, Mary, has had several chest infections but is otherwise well. Both parents, particularly Cathy, are reluctant to have her tested, although she is being seen at the family clinic which they attend at their local hospital, albeit very irregularly.

Rosie is attending a local primary school, but has not settled well and exhibits disturbed behaviour. The teacher has told Cathy that Rosie is aggressive and destructive. Mary goes to the Mildmay nursery three times a week, where her development and clinical condition are being closely watched. Cathy finds it very difficult to think about the future of her children, as this means facing up to the deaths of herself and Eddie. When confronted with these issues, her coping mechanism to date has been denial and oblivion through drugs. She is very distressed when separated from her children, but she often cannot cope with them when they are with her. Both she and Eddie are often 'stoned' by the time the children return home from school in the afternoon, and social workers have from time to time threatened to remove the children from their care.

Cathy has always been a pretty girl, but is now very self-conscious about her appearance as she has lost weight, has widespread skin problems, and has had to have many of her teeth removed as a result of gingivitis and extensive caries. As a result she is anxious about her relationship with Eddie because he has retained his looks and is fitter than she is.

Cathy and Eddie were referred to Mildmay's Family Care Centre by the Social Services. They were in urgent need of respite care and help with their chaotic lifestyle. It was evident that both parents were experiencing a high level of tension as a result of being unable to supplement their methadone with illegal drug use. Eddie was recovering from his first episode of pneumonia and was managing to maintain his weight in spite of erratic food intake. Cathy, however, complained of poor appetite and nausea, and was very anxious about her continued weight loss. Both children were thin and undernourished. Rosie was traumatised by her experience of life so far, and for most of the time she would not communicate with anyone. The nursery staff eventually found out that she could not understand why her parents were always ill, and that she was fed up with it all.

One of the greatest causes of concern for both Cathy and Eddie was the fear they had that Mary might be positive. Cathy said, 'I think she is, really. She keeps on being ill, and Rosie wasn't ill like that when she was little, but then I tell myself, I'm imagining it, but I just cannot have her tested. I'm too frightened that she'll be found to be positive, and I done it to her. I don't think I could live with myself if she was. I didn't know I was HIV positive when I fell for her, if I'd known, I'd have been more careful.'

A complete medical assessment was carried out on Cathy, Eddie and Mary and appropriate drug and symptom control treatments were prescribed for the parents. The drug dependency unit was contacted to assist in the management of their drug use, and their key workers attended a case conference to plan their future drug management. Mary's health was continually monitored by the doctor and nursing team throughout her stay at the Family Centre, to ensure timely responses to any presenting symptoms. A nutritional programme was started, which included small, high calorie, appetising meals for the parents and regular, balanced meals were encouraged for the children. A programme of stress management was introduced for Cathy and Eddie which focused on a number of relaxation techniques. The counsellor and chaplain visited the parents together and separately, and couple counselling around the issues of death and dying were also started.

Cathy and Eddie talked with the doctors and the counsellors about their problems with having Mary tested. Ultimately they decided that they would not have her tested for the moment. They felt that they had enough to cope with, but asked the doctor to keep an eye on her and not 'let anything happen to her'.

In conjunction with the family's social worker, a long-term plan of care was started for the children, which looked at fostering and adoption options, together with schooling and nursery placements. Strategies for addressing the psychological needs of Rosie and Mary were planned by the counselling team, in conjunction with the childcare staff in the Family Care Centre and with all relevant community services.

Over their two-week stay at Mildmay, the family's wellbeing improved as they adopted a more settled lifestyle. Both Eddie and Cathy felt more supported, which resulted in a reduction in their stress. Rosie's behaviour improved as she started to talk to the staff and gain insight into what was happening to her family. The family were put on the urgent waiting list for re-housing, and appropriate benefits were secured. Cathy said, 'The greatest benefit to us in coming here is that we can bring our kids with us. Someone takes Rosie to school and picks her up, so I don't have to worry about her, and although I love little Mary, I just don't want her around when I don't feel well. That makes me feel worse because I feel guilty, but because she can come with me and I don't have to look after her if I'm not up to it, it's just what I need. We won't have much more time together as a family. When I can bring myself to it I'm going to send Rosie and Mary home to my mum, and if we keep on getting ill like we have, that day will come soon.'

This young family had a complex set of health, social, spiritual, psychological and practical needs which are common to families in their position. Their story reinforces the need for family care and highlights the unique problems suffered by children affected by and infected with HIV disease. At least there were now practical ways in which we could help them at Mildmay.

Ann and Jan

Let me tell you of another family, also representative of the varied needs we were having to meet at the Family Care Centre. Ann and her husband Jan are of two different nationalities – neither British. Before Ann came to Britain, she and Jan had both been generally well, but before coming Ann had had a child in her own country who had died shortly after birth.

They came to the UK and soon afterwards Ann became pregnant again and attended ante-natal clinics. She was tested for HIV and found to be positive. She and Jan discussed the possibility of terminating the pregnancy with the social worker at the acute hospital, but together they decided against it.

Ann was initially admitted to Mildmay for respite care and later came for day care. As her pregnancy progressed she was frightened of being alone and feared she would not be strong enough to deliver the baby as she felt very weak. I can remember sitting in the day centre with her and her telling me, 'I will not have the strength to push this baby out when the time comes.'

I said to her, 'The midwife will take care of you and if you are too weak they will make alternative arrangements for you.'

She also told me she was frightened of being in the house alone because she was not feeling well. She had no way of contacting Jan or anyone else in an emergency, and so community support was arranged and a telephone installed in her home in response to her needs.

At term she was admitted to hospital where she had a healthy baby boy by Caesarean section. At eighteen months old as I write, he is still healthy, developing well and achieving his milestones. To date there is no evidence of HIV disease. Ann, however, became increasingly unwell and the family was admitted to the Family Care Centre. Her husband, Jan, had been tested and was found to be HIV positive, but was at that time keeping well. They spent much time together considering the needs of their baby. Ann could not say, 'When I die', but painfully referred to a time 'When I am not here'.

We were able to set up a family conference at the Family Care Centre to consider the way forward for the family. It consisted of Ann, her husband Jan, his mother and her sister. Because of Jan's HIV status, the family decided that it would be better for the child to be brought up in Ann's country by a member of her family there. We found it difficult to understand how the father could bear to be parted from his child, but it was their decision and we respected it.

Staff at Mildmay raised the money for an aunt to come to

England to be with Ann and her husband until Ann died. The aunt stayed in the relatives' suite and started to get to know the nephew she had never met before. The counselling and pastoral care teams worked with the whole family and with the child, who attended the nursery. Jan's family visited regularly and were also a source of great support. They made it clear to Ann that they would look after Jan and care for him when he became sick. Ann seemed to be at peace about the arrangement, but she was not one to show her feelings, and it must have been very hard for her to see her aunt with the child, knowing that she would not see him grow up.

Ann died peacefully, supported by those who loved her, and after the funeral her aunt returned to her home country with her nephew. It may not have been the outcome we would have predicted, but we were privileged to be involved in facilitating the solution of the problem by the family members themselves. The important thing was that Ann's wishes for her child's future were carried out, with the family's agreement about what would be best for him.

Reflections on the Family Care Centre

The extreme fatigue and exhaustion caused by increasing debility and disability as the AIDS condition progresses will inevitably produce their toll on a mother. Trying to care for a young child is exhausting, and yet the mere idea of separation from her child could cause severe distress and affect her general condition. This is where the availability of community care, together with planned and emergency respite care, is crucial. The flexible arrangements that Mildmay introduced as early as 1989 to allow children to accompany their parents for care simply acted as a forerunner to the Family Care Centre, where we could offer much improved facilities. Mothers would otherwise have continued to face an impossible dilemma. The responsibility of a child or children, and the resistance that the mother may have to the child being taken into care, may cause her to delay seeking help for herself. The situation may then become an emergency and result in admission to hospital, with the children being taken into care amidst great trauma.

Thankfully, Mildmay can now act fast in making the necessary arrangements to admit families to the centre. Special attention can be devoted to the child, who may also be infected with the virus, in order to allow the mother adequate periods of rest. Those involved in caring for the child may be paediatric nurses, nursery nurses and play specialists. The care may be extended into the night as appropriate, and the child can be removed to a separate room to avoid the risk of waking the mother, interrupting much-needed sleep. The important thing is that she can feel calm and reassured in the knowledge that her child is close by and is being safely looked after by trained staff. Alternatively, the mother may be supported from the centre to enable her to remain at home for as long as possible, even when suffering bouts of chronic ill health. At times like this she may welcome the opportunity for her child to attend the nursery.

Women are traditionally, of course, the providers of care to their children, husband and parents. It is a sad fact that their sense of commitment to duty is not always reciprocated by the other members. Many, unfortunately, are deserted by their partner on revelation of their diagnosis. Veronica Moss, our Medical Director, once commented in an article: 'The woman who has a partner willing to care for her when she herself is ill, disabled or dying, is indeed fortunate.' ('Terminal Care for Women with Aids', in *Women and HIV*, eds Johnson and Johnstone, Churchill Livingstone, 1993.)

We have seen too many instances where women have been ruthlessly abandoned and left to fend for themselves and their children. In the absence of a partner, the ill woman has serious cause for concern. In countries where the culture of the extended family is very strong, the responsibility for her care will usually pass to her own mother, with the care of the children passing on to the husband's side of the family. This may prove to be an overwhelming burden for a grandmother who may be suffering from the problems attendant with old age. In most countries in the western hemisphere, there may be no one at all to care for the ill woman, who will then inevitably end up in hospital. The care that Mildmay offers, embracing residential care, day care and community liaison support, can go a long way towards alleviating such problems. From the very beginning of our work in the Family Care Centre, over 70 per cent of the families cared for have been mothers who no longer have a partner.

Planning for the future of their children is something that many of the mothers have great difficulty in addressing. In some cultures talking about death is believed to make it happen or hasten it on, and the subject is taboo. We began our family work with one mother who was admitted with a baby to Alexandra Ward, and even then we wanted to involve the mother in choices about the future of her child. This seems obvious from our Western viewpoint. We had thought that to involve mothers in the choice of foster or adopted parents would be the best way to deal with the matter, but quickly found that some mothers could not handle the situation. We found that adoption has to be thought about very carefully, taking into account different cultural attitudes. When we visited Zimbabwe we were told that a mother from there would be unlikely to want her child adopted by another Zimbabwean family. This was because, if any misfortune befell the family, any 'outsider' within the family group would be considered to have caused the problem and might therefore be the first to be blamed and removed from the family group.

In our work with individuals with AIDS we had encountered many whose only way of coping with their illness, even when very sick, was to practise denial. They refused to think about the fact that they had an incurable illness and were going to die sooner rather than later. In my work with cancer patients I had found that many of them used a similar coping mechanism. Often there was collusion in families where someone would not want his or her partner or family member to be told the truth about their diagnosis, because they wanted to protect them. I can remember one family where the wife had ensured that I would not tell her husband the diagnosis on my first visit to the home. As I got to know the family, I realised that even though he had not been told his diagnosis, he had a very good idea of what it was, and I felt that at any time he might ask me outright. I told the wife that I would have great difficulty in feeling justified in lying to him, should he ask me. Eventually she gave me permission to tell him if he did ask me. He did, and when I told him the truth, he burst into tears and said, 'What a relief, now I can stop fighting and start living what is left for me.' When his wife came in, they put their arms around each other and cried together, but those tears were healing and from then onwards there were no secrets between them. They could remember together, plan together, help each other and enjoy the time they had left.

Where it is the patient's wish not to talk about things, their wishes must be respected, but of course it raises particular problems when there is no plan for a child's future. We realised that the care of these children had to be addressed separately from the care of their parents. They were not an appendage to the parent: they had their own needs as individuals and provision had to be made for these as part of the family package.

Who were these children affected by AIDS that we cared for? Many were small children who asked no questions, who had watched their parents change from someone who ran about and played with them to someone who stayed in bed most of the time and could not run, walk or play any more. Many were rude, difficult and irritable, some were often aggressive, disruptive and destructive – and always seeking attention. A large number had the virus themselves. They were often sick and had scratchy skin, coughs and colds, running noses and little energy. Some, even at four years old, were carers. They were looking after a sick parent and in some situations they were the only carer. Then there were the orphans, who had lost their second or only parent. They were cared for usually by other relatives or by foster parents.

We had to learn how to work with these children and their enormous, baffling problems. There was very little experience in this field in the UK and at Mildmay we were privileged to be in at the beginning of family care initiatives. It is my experience that as parents, we are often not very good at addressing, or even acknowledging, the pain of our children. I have been amazed, however, at how much even a very young child can understand. Acknowledging their feelings and involving them in the sadness, rather than protecting them from it, can be supportive and creative, not only for the child but also for the whole family, and seems to build a much surer foundation for the future.

11
A TIME OF
NEW OPPORTUNITIES
1993–4

Further developments

The Family Care Centre was the great achievement of 1993, but that year and the following one were full of other important developments as well. Some may have seemed smaller, but were none the less memorable for that, and we were to find ourselves facing some major new challenges also.

A *welcoming change*

One of the small but important changes was the 'facelift' given to our entrance and reception areas. Having contained expenditure over the years by largely concentrating on the improvement of patient care areas according to its 'patients first' philosophy, Mildmay now had to show a slight change in direction. We may have had first-class facilities inside, but the outside appearance of the building left something to be desired. The shabby canopy over the entrance had to go.

There was also the need to ensure a warm, attractive, design co-ordinated environment in which to welcome patients and make them feel comfortable upon arrival for admission. The need to improve the reception area had been highlighted for me by Martyn Lewis when he had come to chair one of Mildmay's conferences. When I told him of our 'patients first' policy, he said, 'But if this is the first time you have visited Mildmay and you are feeling apprehensive anyway, don't you think it will be important for your first impression to be one of warmth and comfort, rather than stark but clean worn out chairs and plain green walls?' He was so right and the main reception was duly upgraded and refurbished, the colour co-ordination, pictures and furnishings again being suggested by an architect. It really did make such a difference.

Friends and family

It was not only patients we were welcoming into our reception area either. There were also some very special visitors to be catered for at times. A major donor to the Family Care Centre in 1993 was the Chaplin family. Charlie Chaplin never made it to Mildmay, but two of his children did. We were delighted to welcome Geraldine and Eugene Chaplin to tea at the hospital. They had come on behalf of the Chaplin family as a whole to make a £70,000 donation towards the capital costs of Mildmay's Family Care Centre.

The descendants of William Pennefather, the founder of Mildmay, also contacted us. We invited them to visit the new Mildmay and to have lunch with us. They told us some wonderful stories and we described to them how Mildmay had developed. They then let us know that William Pennefather was to make a grand return to the hospital – somewhat surprising, some one hundred and twenty years on! It was in the form of a framed portrait of the great man, fondly referred to as 'Holy Willie' by his descendants. This was presented to us by Sheila Pennefather, the wife of William's great-grandson. It was given pride of place in Mildmay's boardroom.

Fundraising

It was marvellous to have such individual gestures of support and we needed all the encouragement available. There was, of course, a continual demand for funds which somehow we had to find. During this time there were some changes to our fundraising structures.

Mildmay was now all AIDS and the former League of Friends decided it was time for them to move on and set up a charity more in keeping with their aim to serve the local community. We were grateful to them for the many years of support that they had given. They had brought comfort to patients and staff alike by the allocation of monies which they had raised. Their departure left a gap which was then filled by the formation of the Friends of Mildmay, created as a new charity to work with the hospital in the provision of support, help and fundraising activities.

There was also a need for essential investment in Mildmay's future. The Appeal Committee was no longer in existence since the end of the Centenary Appeal in 1993, and the only staff remaining in fundraising were those who had worked for the Appeal. There was a real need to review the activities of that department. We had paid a consultancy firm to provide a fund-raiser to work with the staff on a temporary basis: we employed them to also review the work of the department and to make recommendations regarding our future fundraising strategy. As a result we appointed a Head of Public Affairs, whose responsi-bility it was to develop the fundraising and publicity with short- and long-term strategies. There was still about £1 million of the £3.3 million needed to pay off the Family Care Centre, although it was remarkable how God had provided for us. Charity dona-tions were then at an all time low and, of course, on top of that some people will not give to AIDS charities.

Further expansion

Despite fundraising difficulties, we still had to meet the demands of a constant increase in the numbers of new patients. Pressure on our beds was increasing in proportion. The three main wards now had a total of twenty-eight beds and the first six beds of the Family Care Centre had been opened. We could not meet demands for our beds on the three wards and in the Family Care Centre. The directors therefore decided that the unfinished work on the second floor of the Family Care Centre would have to be finished as a matter of urgency, to enable us to open a further six beds.

Another possibility also being considered was to develop a further four bedrooms at the end of Alexandra Ward which had been left vacant when the day centre moved. We made a bid to the Regional Health Authority to see if they would be prepared to fund the cost of refurbishing that area. The cost was estimated to be £250,000, but the increase in the number of beds would reduce the unit cost per bed per day. The Regional Health Authority agreed and the work proceeded.

We now found ourselves in the position of being able to purchase two plots of valuable land on the Hackney Road, which formed the frontage of Mildmay's existing property. Two years earlier, when we had enquired about the cost of the land, it had been in excess of £500,000. Due to the recession and dramatic reductions in the price of land and property, we were now being offered the land for £185,000. We were successful in acquiring an interest-free loan for the land, to be repaid when we could afford it. We were so pleased we had waited: God's timing is always perfect and we needed to be reminded of this sometimes, when we would have raced ahead in our enthusiasm and eagerness to get things done.

Meeting the challenge of the marketplace

The development of a new-style NHS, with its commercialised world of purchasers, providers and contracts, had forced radical changes for everyone in the business of health and social care. Gone was the safety net of government ringfenced funding for AIDS care, which had ensured that the amounts of money devoted to the AIDS cause could not be diverted elsewhere. As a result, Mildmay now faced the challenge and uncertainty of competing for contracts for its services in order to survive. It was one of the biggest challenges we faced at that time, and was to be an ongoing point of anxiety.

Mildmay quickly positioned itself at the forefront of the effort to meet the new NHS directives by investing in two key appointments. The first was a Business Development Manager, responsible for negotiating the contracts with purchasers; the

second was a Quality Facilitator, who would develop, throughout the organisation, a strategy to ensure that a high quality
service was both maintained and documented. Since 1989, when
Mildmay was nominated the model for AIDS hospice care, we
had aimed to remain at the leading edge in the years to come by
offering a quality-led, value-for-money service which ensured
that limited resources were used in the most efficient and
effective way. The combination of these elements, however,
demanded a formidable balancing act.

The NHS reforms were now forcing Mildmay into a rethink
of the value-for-money aspects. The reforms continued to have
wide-ranging implications, both for units within the NHS and
those outside it. Independently run Mildmay, as a provider unit
to the NHS, proved to be no exception and was forced to
undertake a major re-organisation of its nursing grade structure.
The nursing structure which had been adopted almost six years
before used an unequivocally generous ratio of highly trained
nursing staff to patients. This was because the nurses were
entering a new arena of care and we needed them to evaluate
their practice continually. Only trained nurses were qualified to
do this. Now, however, there were more nurses with experience
and training in caring for people with AIDS, gained not only at
Mildmay, but also in acute hospitals, community and voluntary
services, and in centres of education. The situation had changed.
Sadly and unavoidably there were a few redundancies. 'So much
for progress . . .': the NHS reforms proved to be costlier than
we had imagined.

The fact is that it is expensive to care for people with AIDS.
In order to remain competitive within the new market culture,
however, it was essential that we reduced our costs without
compromising the quality of our services. Cost improvement
initiatives therefore became the responsibility of each department within the hospital. Looking back over the years, I believe
that one of the factors that has ensured our success has been
that we have always been prepared for change. We had been
pro-active in planning for change in a number of ways, for
example, the development of the computer programme which

enabled us to provide much improved information about our services. This professional approach is, I believe, essential for hospices who are trying to attract statutory funding. The development of information technology became essential in any case as the organisation grew. Bruce Levitan, Mildmay's first computer manager, planned the development and set up more than forty PCs, all of them networked together so that information could be moved around with ease between all departments. The I.T. programme began to improve efficiency and output and an assistant was eventually appointed to manage the growing work. A hospital information system now allows Mildmay's interdisciplinary team to record, share and analyse information about the care patients receive, and to monitor results and standards. The hospital also has to collect activity data for the purchases of our services.

Mildmay's entry into the NHS marketplace was officially marked by the launch of its new Business Prospective in an open day for prospective purchasers. On the eve of the launch we received a message of encouragement from Dr Kenneth Calman, the Chief Medical Officer at the Department of Health. 'I am delighted to support the patient focused approach to the care of people with AIDS at Mildmay Mission Hospital,' he wrote. 'My visits to Mildmay over the last few years have demonstrated to me the commitment and caring attitude of staff and their dedication to those they serve. Their concern for children and families is of a particular interest to me, as it recognises this important aspect of the care of those with HIV infection.'

With the advent of these changes, however, there was a cost to the organisation in terms of staff morale. Having witnessed the redundancies which, in the event, were voluntary and not compulsory, some staff were feeling insecure. Even as Christians, many of them found they had anxieties which they had difficulty in overcoming. It was little reassurance to realise that staff in the NHS itself were going through similar, if not more radical, changes and there were redundancies at every level. We did our best to assist staff in coping with the insecurity, although we could not take it away, no matter how much we wanted to.

As Mildmay has grown and become increasingly competitive, many people have had difficulty with the fact that we had become an 'organisation', a 'business', a 'provider unit'. The jargon seemed uncomfortable, especially when we had to speak of providing 'packages of care'. At Board level, however, we knew we had to lead rather than follow these new developments. We had to be ready to adjust and change, if need be, to protect God's investment in His work at Mildmay.

Part of being prepared to make hard decisions and accept changes was that we had to face sensibly the need to make some of the staff redundant. Having already experienced this situation with the closure of Mathieson Ward in 1991, it was very traumatic for both staff managers and the organisation as a whole. We have been criticised by some for making staff redundant, because they feel that as a Christian organisation we should not behave in that way. I believe, however, that we have a responsibility to behave in a professional as well as caring manner, and we are subject to the same market forces as any other provider unit, whether NHS or not. We must be seen to provide an efficient value-for-money service, and we must always be ready to do what is necessary to ensure the survival of our services to people with AIDS. In my experience this has all too often meant that unpopular decisions have had to be made.

Causes for joy

In the midst of a general feeling of gloom, two things happened to lighten our load. One was an honour given to me; the other was a very special event for two of our patients.

My experience of working at Mildmay – at a job I really enjoyed doing and which afforded me exciting opportunities and challenges – was in itself very rewarding. When I was awarded a Fellowship of the Royal College of Nursing, on 19th October 1994, I was amazed to receive such a public honour, and simply felt that God was so generous to me. The citation read:

Ruth Sims has demonstrated innovation and originality in palliative care nursing, in particular her outstanding work with people with AIDS at the Mildmay Mission Hospital in Hackney, London. Her vision of patient-directed care has become a model for nursing in this field. Recognised nationally and internationally the Mildmay has become a world-renowned centre of excellence in the care of people with AIDS under her direction.

For her outstanding contribution to palliative nursing care, particularly for people with AIDS, and her promotion and development of education in this field, Council confers this Fellowship of the Royal College of Nursing.

This award was terribly exciting for me, but a wedding that took place in May 1994 broke new ground even for Mildmay, for it was no ordinary couple. The bride and groom had both been attending Mildmay's day centre for over a year and they were both HIV positive. The wedding preparations inevitably bore a strong Mildmay flavour. Several members of Mildmay staff lent a hand, their involvement including dress fittings, catering, flowers, decorations, photography and transport. Debbie, the day centre's occupational therapist, helped Mary get ready for the big day. For the short journey to church, she was accompanied in the Mildmay car by her proud father, who had travelled down from Scotland for the occasion. The ceremony took place at Shoreditch Church, which is next door to Mildmay, and Nigel, Mildmay's Anglican chaplain, officiated. The reception was held back at Mildmay in Buxton Hall, but there came a time when enough was enough, so for their honeymoon in Tenerife there was no Mildmay person in sight!

Developments in Uganda

These small joys, however, could be said to have been somewhat eclipsed by the excitement of developing links between Uganda and Mildmay in 1993 and 1994. The successful training course in Kenya in 1992 was followed in 1993 by the first course to be conducted in Uganda, with another course planned for Tanzania. We trained thirty-two senior health care professionals in Uganda and during our visit there we met the Director General of the Uganda AIDS Commission again. We had first met the Honourable Manuel Pinto in 1991 at the reception given by the British High Commissioner. He was the MP for Rakai District, the worst hit area of Uganda in terms of AIDS. During our 1993 visit, I remember talking with him over dinner one evening about the HIV epidemic in Uganda. I said to him, 'It is going to take a power greater than the willpower of individuals to change behaviour and control the epidemic in Africa, and I believe that power to be the power given by God.' He had agreed with me and had also gone on to say, 'We need help in this country to care for people as well as programmes of prevention.' This meeting was to have an amazing outcome!

Manuel Pinto was next encountered at an International Conference in Edinburgh where he met with Veronica Moss, our Medical Director. He said something quite astounding and it was this: 'We want to give Mildmay some land so that you can come out to build and manage a care centre for us, so that people with AIDS can be helped.'

Veronica returned from Edinburgh very excited and told me about this. Nonetheless, we told ourselves it might be a long time before we heard anything more. In my Board report a couple of days later, I wrote, 'I believe that now we should have a time of consolidation of our services with no major capital developments to be pursued in the near future.' As I wrote it I thought, 'Thank you, Lord, I can really do with a rest.'

Two days later, I went into the office to be met by Dorothy Hannan, my PA, who said, 'You are not going to believe this, come quickly, I've been waiting to show you this.' She handed me a fax from Manuel Pinto in which he offered Mildmay a two-and-a-half-acre plot of land on Mbuya Hill (on the outskirts of Kampala) to build an AIDS Care and Study Centre. He urged us to visit Uganda as soon as possible to discuss details. This fax was then followed very quickly by an official letter saying that the Kampala City Council had allocated two and a half acres of land to the Uganda AIDS Commission, which they in turn would like to give to Mildmay to build the proposed Mildmay Centre.

I could hardly believe it. My chance for a rest, however, was out of the window. I was so excited by this wonderful opportunity – what a privilege! From a small concern in a little back street in the East End of London had developed a work with credibility in both Christian and secular circles, endorsed by both royalty and government. Now here we were receiving an invitation from the government of Uganda. It seemed clear to me why all this had happened: because it was God's work, I believed, we were experiencing miracle after miracle. He had helped us to equip and resource our activities, and was now indicating that He wanted to expand Mildmay's work further still.

We did not feel overwhelmed by this new task. We did not worry over the fact that we had no experience at all of developing a satellite unit, let alone one in Africa, or contemplate what it might mean to obtain funding, oversee a building project and establish a service, having designed the operational plan and recruited suitable staff. With God's help, we knew we only had to take one step at a time. It is often such a blessing that we cannot see into the future! Veronica and I immediately set to work on a preliminary project proposal so that we would have a discussion tool when we went to Africa.

Our first step after that was for Mrs Taylor Thompson, Veronica and I to go to Uganda, meet with the Uganda AIDS Commission and see the land on offer. We were taken by staff from the Commission to visit the site on Mbuya Hill. We were certainly not experts on the suitability of land and we realised that we would have to find someone to help us in this area.

We had many contacts in Uganda by now because of our training programmes, and we knew the staff who ran the AIDS clinics at the government and non-government hospitals in and around Kampala. We had been to clinics and seen how little was on offer. We had seen that people were dying from symptoms that we would find so easy to treat in the West, and not always with expensive medicine. We had visited one hospital where we saw approximately three hundred people waiting to be seen in the AIDS outpatients clinic. The clinic started at 1.00 p.m. and we were told that it was unlikely to finish before 7.00 p.m. There was one full-time, one part-time and two voluntary doctors to see the patients, and everywhere we went the story was the same: there was an overwhelming demand for care. We therefore had some idea of the size of the problem, and when talking with the doctors concerned with AIDS, we had a little first-hand experience to help us make appropriate judgments.

Although we had prepared our preliminary proposal, we realised that we were not the best people to decide alone what sort of care facility was needed. We also had to consult with local health care professionals and people with AIDS. Unlike the situation in the UK, however, few people with AIDS in Uganda would have been prepared to offer suggestions, for cultural reasons. We formed a local advisory committee made up of professionals involved in AIDS work, spearheaded by the fifteen Ugandan AIDS Commissioners. We made sure they understood that our experience was in the care of people with advanced HIV disease and that we were not primarily involved in prevention or the support of those with asymptomatic HIV disease.

After a number of discussions, a Memorandum of Understanding between Mildmay Mission Hospital and the Government of Uganda was signed. Mildmay agreed to pay the lease for the land and to develop on it a palliative care centre for people with AIDS. This was still subject to discussion and agreement by the rest of the Mildmay Board.

Our visit was only a week long, and what a week it was! We met the Minister of Health, the Honourable Dr James Makumbi, who arranged for us to meet with the President of Uganda, His Excellency Yoweri Museveni. They were both very enthusiastic about our project and promised to help in any way that they could. The President offered us exemption from local and import tax, which was an enormous contribution to make.

Dr Makumbi was to become not only my personal friend but a great supporter of our work. He advised us that Mr Jagdish, Director of the World Bank, was in Kampala visiting that week, and asked if we would like to meet him. We went with Dr Makumbi at the appointed time and, although the meeting lasted only thirty minutes, we left with the promise of $250,000 (US dollars) and encouragement to return for more money if we established links with Makerere University and the Joint Clinical Research Council, to whose work in AIDS the World Bank was already contributing.

During the week we also paid a second visit to Mbuya Hill. While we were looking round, the Finance and Administrative Manager of the Uganda AIDS Commission, Mr James Mukasa, told us that the Bible College at the top of the hill had been built by a local builder. He asked if we would like to see it, and we drove up there. Just as we arrived, the Director of the College was getting into his car to leave, but kindly stopped to ask if he could help us. When we told him what we were doing, he got out of his car and offered to show us around. He told us that he had entrusted the building of the College to a Norwegian builder who, with his Ugandan wife, had lived in Uganda for many years. His name was Björn Simensen. He told us that Björn was honest and trustworthy and had taken over the site at the commencement of the building work, managing the construction until he had handed over the key of a finished building.

The building was just the kind that would be appropriate to our needs. We were told where we could contact Mr Simensen and decided that we would try to see him before we returned home to Britain. Before we could even organise this, he presented himself at our hotel a few hours later. We talked with him about our invitation and showed him our project proposal, arranging to go and see him for further discussions at his office. He was a Christian, and as we told him more details about our project and our work in London, he became very interested and offered to help us in any way that he could.

When we returned to Britain we thought about others who

might help us with the building side of the project. The first person who came to mind was Mr Greville Mitchell, who had been a generous benefactor to Mildmay already. He was our honorary site consultant and a close friend. It was wonderful when Greville not only agreed to advise from a distance, but was also willing to travel out to Uganda, funding his own expenses, and to work with me on the project as required. How grateful we were that this very busy man should be led by God to work with us and, as we found out later, to give of his money as well as of his time.

When Greville visited Uganda, he arranged for a site survey and a detailed soil analysis. To cut a long story short, he found out that the site on Mbuya Hill was quite unsuitable for our purpose. Björn had been talking to people who lived locally and found out that it had, in fact, been a large crater which had been filled over the years with rubbish, had become grassed over and had then been planted with cassava and other crops. Now, after rain, it was seeping what was thought to be toxic waste. A second site was offered nearby, but again had to be rejected. Finally, we decided to look into the possibility of buying private land.

While we were busy trying to identify a suitable site, we were also endeavouring to get Mildmay registered as a Ugandan non-government organisation (NGO). That really was easier said than done. We spent hours waiting in corridors and outside doors, and eventually persistence won the day. We were seen and, with the help of the Director General of the Uganda AIDS Commission and the Chairman of the Ugandan NGO committee, we were able to get our registration through in time for us to be able to purchase land for the site.

Björn helped us again. He told us of some land which was available for sale in a prime position on the Entebbe Road, six kilometres outside Kampala. This road runs from Entebbe airport to Kampala and is one of the main roads with very good access and public transport services. The site was on Naziba Hill in Lubowa and it had frontage onto the Entebbe Road. Greville had all the necessary preliminary investigations, including the sinking of a bore hole, undertaken and they all proved satisfactory. Having undertaken a great deal of work for which he had paid out of his own pocket, Greville then told Mildmay that he would donate the money for the purchase of the land from the Andrew Mitchell Christian Charitable Trust, which he had set up in memory of his son. And so we bought seven and a half acres of land on the hill. It was a place of beauty and tranquillity and our prayer was that the people we would care for there would find comfort and hope.

From then on I made frequent trips out to Uganda, often accompanied by a Director of the Mildmay Board so that they could familiarise themselves with the situation there, meet key people and gain an understanding of the project. Meetings of the steering committee took place and the project proposal was finalised. Normally we would have submitted bids for funding to several donor agencies, but in this instance I had a strong conviction that we should only approach one potential donor, and that was the Overseas Development Administration (ODA). The ODA had funded our training programmes in East and Central Africa and as a result I had met some of the staff there. We therefore submitted a project proposal to the ODA with a request for £2 million to fund the capital costs of the project.

How do you manage a unit by remote control? I don't know, but I know a man who does! It has always seemed important to me to acknowledge limitations and solicit help as necessary when attempting new spheres of work. I am grateful that God has given me an optimistic outlook on life – it has helped me so much when confronting mountains! I can honestly say that I have never felt alone when facing changes and new challenges. I certainly know that I would never have dared to make recommendations concerning Mildmay's future if I had not known that God was with me and my fellow directors to give us wisdom and guide our thinking. Decisions at Mildmay are seldom made unilaterally, but with Mildmay Uganda, the Board knew I would often need to make an 'on-the-spot' decision when out there by myself. At these times I felt very upheld by prayer – the prayers of the Board, my fellow directors, the staff, my house group and prayer chain, and other friends and family members. I was confident that with God's help I would be able to lead the developments in Uganda, especially as Greville had promised to oversee the building work and Veronica, our Medical Director, was to develop the clinical side of the work. I was also confident that we would be given the funding for the project. I was not certain whether the ODA would give us the full amount, but I was sure that it would be given to us in some way.

A *mountainous challenge*

Planning and running the Mildmay Centre in Uganda was perhaps the biggest challenge we had yet faced. The enormity of it was brought home to me again and again on my repeated visits to the country.

During one of my visits I was taken out with the Home Care Team from the Nsambya Hospital, Kampala. Nsambya Hospital is an NGO run by the Catholic Church. The team consisted of a driver who is also a counsellor, together with a social worker and a nurse. The first patient we saw was a young girl of twenty-three who was clearly in the terminal phase of the disease. Her mother was caring for her and she lay in a small mud and wattle hut, on grass and a reed mat with no mattress. She was painfully thin and obviously dehydrated, complaining of painful diarrhoea and cramps, weakness and lethargy. She was not eating because she had oral candida and, whenever she ate anything, it would start off the diarrhoea again and she would cry out in pain. She was also feverish. The team spent a long time talking with this patient and her mother. The nurse increased the dose of the anti-diarrhoeal agent she was taking and advised her to eat little and often. I was surprised they did not encourage fluids but saw it as more important that she ate food. They did suggest, however, that the mother should boil rice and give the patient the rice water to drink, which would help the diarrhoea. The hut was small, dark and smoky and the nurse suggested that the girl be taken out into the fresh air. The team helped her to walk outside, which she did with great difficulty, and then she lay down on a rush mat under a tree. It was thought that she might not live for many more days.

The second patient we saw was called Alice, who was twenty-five years old. Around her were her mother, her sister and babies, as well as her brother who was visiting. Her own baby was twenty-two months old and also ill. The consultation took place outside the mud and wattle hut, where the family were all sitting in the shade preparing cassava. Alice was eating some matoke with gravy and the green vegetables which are common in this area. It was then just about 1.00 p.m. and she told us that this was the first food her mother had prepared for her. She said that her mother did not look after her properly, but when the team challenged the mother, she laughed and said that Alice was telling lies: she did feed and look after her properly. We also examined the sick baby. She had the typical skin rash, with a fever, and looked very ill and dark around the eyes. The baby was refusing to eat or drink and had a cough. As we left, the team told me that they believed Alice's report that her mother was not looking after her properly, but there was little they could do.

We then visited Lawrence, who was in his forties and very sick. He was at a neighbour's hut when we arrived and his little cement-brick house was locked up. We waited for him to come back and he looked typical of many of the sick patients we have in Mildmay. He was emaciated and had difficulty in walking, even with a stick. It was almost lunchtime and he told us that he had had nothing to eat that day because the jet on his little stove was broken. Asked if he had any family, he said, 'No'. His sons were in the army, he was divorced from his wife and no one was looking after him. The team felt it a matter of priority to get the stove fixed and so it was taken away. He took us inside his house, where he had a bed and a mattress. Everything was tidy and what few belongings he had were obviously cared for. There was even a bowl with a scrubbing brush and a bar of soap by it. He said that, if only his stove were repaired, he could look after himself. All the patients were given powdered milk, rice, a loaf of bread and some sugar, but I felt very sad about Lawrence because he had nobody to look after him, and I wondered what would happen when he could no longer get out and about. It was remarkable that he was still moving about, but I suppose he had no alternative.

The next patient we saw was a young girl in her early twenties called Betty. She had been turned out by her husband when she was found to have AIDS and he had kept the children. Betty was desperate to have them visit her, but he was refusing to bring them. When the team had visited Betty the previous week, she had been very sick with abdominal pain and diarrhoea, but they had given her some antacids and an anti-diarrhoeal medication, and this week she was feeling much better. Betty had been out, cultivating her father's land. When her mother had died, her father and brother had turned to alcohol and were always drinking. When Betty's husband sent her away, she went back to her father, who abused her physically and told her she was a prostitute and that she was to get out of his house. So Betty had hired a room in a house not far from her father, for a thousand Ugandan shillings (60 pence) a month.

When Betty felt well enough she would go and cultivate her father's land. Recently, however, her father and brother would arrive in the evening, drunk and demanding food. She felt that, as a person with AIDS who was often sick, she had to conserve what little food she had in order to look after herself if she became sick again. She had been to the 'parish council' of village elders to tell them about her situation, but they merely told her she had to return home as her father and brother were on their own and she had a responsibility to look after them. This seemed such a hopeless situation, but at least she looked quite well physically and seemed in quite good spirits despite everything.

Since the rainy season is the time to cultivate land, and Uganda had had some rain, Betty was sowing beans in order to have a crop and vegetables to sell in approximately two months. Cassava and sweet potatoes take six months to ripen, and maize four months, so beans are a good crop if money is needed quickly. Betty had everything tidily placed, with supplies of groundnuts, beans, eggplant and cassava, so she looked as if she was managing to trade and get some food. Her greatest unhappiness was that she could not see her children and this unhappiness was, she felt, spoiling her life.

Our final visit was to Annette. Her husband had died of AIDS and he had had three other wives and seventeen children altogether. Aged twenty-seven, Annette had six children of her own but was looking after seven children in her small mud and wattle cottage, set a long way off the main road along a bumpy dirt track. Her husband had had four homes and this one was the last remaining. The other houses had been taken over by his brothers. His other children were living with a relative, but Annette was helping to support them through the food she sold from her own homestead, where she was raising chickens and growing cassava, sweet potatoes, bananas and vegetables. She also had a small calf and a cow. An uncle was helping her to pay school fees for four of the seven children. Annette had been feverish a few days ago and had walked to the clinic at Nsambya, which was a walk of several hours. She had been given an injection there and was now feeling better. She allowed us to take some photographs of her with her children in front of the house, but she insisted on going to change her dress into the *gomez*, the traditional Ugandan dress with puff sleeves. Again here was another impressive woman who was doing her very best in extremely difficult circumstances and was clearly proud of what she was achieving.

I was also proud to be part of Mildmay's involvement with these people. We had so much to offer in terms of experience and medical knowledge. The Mildmay Centre in Uganda could not be built soon enough.

12

A TIME FOR MORE MIRACLES
1995

A *new year*

The developing project in Uganda took up a great deal of our time and attention, and as we took each step, we realised again and again how God's power could make things possible. Back home in Britain, the story was the same, and at the beginning of 1995, the work was going from strength to strength.

The final work on the second floor of the Family Care Centre had now been finished, new staff had been appointed and we were ready to admit patients. There were now four more rooms on Alexandra Ward and they were also ready to be used. This meant that we now had a total of forty-four beds, plus accommodation for any family members accompanying patients. The day centre and nursery were also in great demand and we had to expand the nursery service from five to seven days a week, remaining open from 8.00 a.m. to 8.00 p.m.

The Education Department had been upgraded with the creation of a new classroom and was now called the Centre for Advanced Studies. There were a number of recognised and approved courses being conducted regularly. All were fully subscribed and we never had to advertise for places. Links were being established with centres of higher education with a view to offering degree-level modules at Mildmay, but first we felt it was time for a review of the Centre's work. This would enable us to identify the best way forward in the light of Mildmay's growth and the new international demands as well as changing educational strategies within independent units and in the NHS.

The library in its new situation in the old boardroom was

also increasingly popular. Mary Spence, our Librarian, had developed the service from merely a 'room with books', to a centre equipped to a very high professional standard, offering books, periodicals, journals, videos, and facilities for literature searches with good links with larger libraries.

Mildmay's steady growth had meant that the staff establishment had increased from thirty people in 1987 to over two hundred and thirty-eight by 1995. A second consultant had been appointed to cope with the increased workload of the medical team. Our office accommodation was stretched to capacity. To release essential space in the main hospital area, my office, together with those of my PA and the staff of the Public Affairs and Communication department, had been moved into staff flats in the remaining part of Sir Graham Rowlandson House in Austin Street.

In 1986 Dr Veronica Moss and Dr M. Foyle, a Consultant Psychiatrist, had planned and set up the Missionaries and Volunteers Health Service (MVHS) within Mildmay to provide medical consultancy and advice to those going out to or returning from overseas service. This service expanded very quickly at the same time as Mildmay's AIDS work was developing. Dr Moss relinquished responsibility for it to concentrate on the AIDS work in 1989, and it became a charity in its own right under the direction of Dr Ted Lankester, working with nurse Jackie Hall. As a separate charity, MVHS rented nine rooms on the third floor of the Mildmay building. MVHS was eventually renamed Interhealth and established a high reputation, expanding its services until the area on the third floor became inadequate for its growing needs. By 1995 it was serving more than ninety missionary societies and aid agencies and it has recently moved to Partnership House in Waterloo. The site it occupied at Mildmay has been refurbished to accommodate me as Chair and Managing Director of Mildmay International along with my staff.

The book written by Veronica Moss and myself on terminal care for people with AIDS had sold well since it was published in 1991, but now needed updating. We had worked on this in

1994 and had expanded it to such an extent that the publishers decided to bring out a new edition of the book, entitled *Palliative Care for People with AIDS*. The new chapters included such topics as caring for drug users with AIDS, caring for women and children, and caring where resources are limited, i.e. in developing countries. The book was published in January 1995 and proved to be a valuable resource for the trainers on our courses in East and Central Africa.

During this year Dr Veronica Moss and I also both received recognition and honour for the work that had been developed at Mildmay. We were very conscious, however, that the development of the services at Mildmay were not due to individuals, but had been the result of team effort. Nonetheless, we were grateful to receive these awards for the glory that could be reflected to God, to Mildmay's services and to the staff of Mildmay, and for the awareness that was created through them of the needs of people with AIDS.

Veronica was awarded the Membership of the Royal College of Physicians (MRCP) for her pioneering work in AIDS palliative medicine. She was the first doctor in this field to be given such a great honour, and only the fourth palliative care doctor ever to receive this award. To my amazement, having already received the Fellowship of the Royal College of Nursing (FRCN) in 1993, I was notified that I was to be given an OBE in the Queen's Birthday Honours List. Feeling that the work was enough of a reward in itself for me, I was glad to receive such an honour: the glory was for God, who had equipped and enabled me for the work He had given me to do.

Africa – great steps forward

For me, however, the great highlights of 1995 took place in Africa. More training courses met with success, and our centre in Uganda was making progress.

Having conducted training courses in both Kenya and Uganda, we were now invited to go to Tanzania to conduct one there. The venue in Moshi was wonderful, near the foot of

Mount Kilimanjaro. Whilst there, we visited Kilimanjaro Christian Medical Centre (KCMC), which had recently been returned from government control back into Christian hands. It was good to be able to give colleagues there a word of encouragement as they set about developing services which had become very run down through lack of financial resources. The course participants at Moshi were very enthusiastic and creative, and all of us – facilitators as well as participants, shared and learned much.

The Chairman of Mildmay, Lord McColl, his wife, Veronica Moss, Dorothy Hannan and myself went to Uganda in May to attend the ground breaking ceremony for Mildmay Uganda. Mr Greville Mitchell, our Honorary Site Consultant, and Lisa, his wife, met us there. Dorothy and I had the task of organising this event and were grateful for the help of the Uganda AIDS Commission and the ODA. The ceremony was held at the site on Naziba Hill on Thursday 25th May. The site had been cleared and fenced by Björn Simensen, who had by then become a great friend and supporter. On the day before the ceremony the large iron gates were manually lifted into place and an enormous hoarding, which read: 'Mildmay Uganda, Palliative Care, Research and Advanced Study Centre', was erected. We prayed for a dry day for the ceremony, as at that time there were rains on a daily basis.

The next day dawned bright and sunny. Telephone communication was tricky, so I had to go to the site to check that everything was in order prior to the event, which was due to start at 2.00 p.m. I found chaos: the canopies had been put up the wrong way round, the caterers had not arrived as promised and there were no chairs for the visitors. In spite of all this, the music from the African Children's Choir as they practised, and the willing smiles of plenty of helpers, created a sense of calm and somehow I remained unruffled. Fred, our driver, drove me to the hotel to find out why no chairs had been delivered, and we were told that they had been cancelled because the hotel had no transport for them. I begged them to get the chairs out immediately and wipe them down, and we promised to send a driver within thirty minutes. Fred then whizzed to the market place, where he left us in the car to go to negotiate a price for a van.

'If they see you,' he said, 'you will be charged *mazungu* (white people) prices! I will be able to negotiate a better price.' He did so, came back, I said, 'Done,' and off he went to give the instructions.

On the way back to the house where we were staying, we passed the flower shop which was meant to be supplying arrangements for the event. Although they should have been picked up two hours earlier, I thought I would just check for safety's sake. The flowers were still there, so I took them with me. By the time I got back to the house, everyone was ready and it was almost time to depart again. When we got to the site an hour later, the sun was still shining in a clear blue sky, gentle music was being relayed across the site, the canopies and chairs were in place, the caterers were standing smartly to attention and all was well.

Many important people attended the ceremony besides Mildmay's own contingency. Our special guests included the Deputy British High Commissioner, the Director of the British Council, Dr Peter Thompson of the ODA, the Archbishop of Uganda and the Minister of Health, the Honourable Dr James Makumbi, our guest of honour who was to conduct the ground breaking ceremony. The African Children's Choir, whom I had first heard singing on British television and who had kindly consented to sing for us, added greatly to the occasion with their inspirational singing.

During my speech I told Dr Makumbi how grateful to God we were that he was alive and well and able to be with us. Some weeks previously, on an earlier trip to Uganda, I had been met at the airport by our driver who said, 'Mama Ruth, we have some terrible news: the Minister of Health is missing and is feared dead, his car was found abandoned by the side of the road and he has not been seen since.'

I had been so upset. Not only had this man been so supportive of Mildmay's project, but on my last visit to him, just a few weeks earlier, he had said to me, 'You are my friend, Ruth.' I felt so sad to be losing my new friend so soon.

The next day the Minister had still not been found, and that evening I rang Mildmay. I asked them to pray that this man's life would be spared and I asked them to contact my church fellowship which was meeting that evening, in order that they too could pray. In Uganda we spent a long time praying. Dr Makumbi had been missing for four days by then and, as the days passed, fear for his life increased. We went to bed that night after our prayers and woke the next morning to the news that Dr Makumbi had been found alive and, although he was not very well, he was not in danger.

When I spoke to him some time afterwards, he told me that he had given up hope of ever being released by the rebels who had captured him. On the morning in question he told me he knew that there was nothing he could say or do that would influence his captors. He said he knew that it had taken a power greater than any in this world to have brought about his release. He had asked me to thank people for their prayers and so it was very special that he was with us that day, to celebrate the launch of a project that had the potential to do so much for people with AIDS in Uganda as well as in other parts of Africa.

As part of the ceremony the land on Naziba Hill was consecrated by the Archbishop of Uganda and Bishop Misaeri Kauma. It was dedicated to God's use with the prayer that, 'Through this Project, His work, God would show His love and care for people with AIDS'.

A spadeful of soil was turned over by Dr Makumbi, after which he unveiled a brass plaque commemorating the occasion. The sky was still blue, the sun was still shining brightly, and there was a refreshing breeze as the choir sang their final song, 'Amazing Grace'. We were so grateful to God that Mildmay had been invited to develop such a greatly needed work in this beautiful country.

At exactly the same time in London, a time difference of two hours, the staff of Mildmay on Hackney Road were also celebrating the launch of Mildmay Uganda. Mildmay's President,

Helen Taylor Thompson, planted a giant rose tree in the front garden there. Members of staff were joined by children from the nursery in laying stones around the tree in symbolic celebration. The stones had been painted in yellow, red and black, the national colours of Uganda. In the warmth of the midday sun, there were prayers of dedication, toasts in celebration and a rousing rendition of the Gospel song, '*Siy Hambe*' (we are marching in the light of God). Last on the menu in London came a Ugandan-style meal, including matoke and groundnut sauce. It was quite a novelty for many of those present! A very high percentage of our patients in the Family Care Centre come from Uganda, however, and earlier in the year, Sharon Hilley, the Catering Manager, who prepared the meal, had been seconded by the catering company to come with us to Uganda to learn how to cook Ugandan food.

Rakai

So we were all learning about Ugandan life and culture. During my frequent visits there, I was becoming very familiar with the country and its people. The AIDS crisis was reaching desperate proportions, but there was an enormous amount of determination to meet and combat the problem.

Rakai is one of the worst-hit areas for AIDS in Uganda. One in three people there are infected with the disease and everyone is affected by it. In order to encourage development of initiatives, the Uganda Women's Effort to Save Orphans (UWESO) had set up a competition to find the best income-generating projects relating to communities' efforts to help orphans. Eleven areas across Uganda had submitted projects and applied to take part. I was invited to accompany the judges in Rakai and seized the chance to see what positive steps were being taken. The outcome of UWESO's work will be that independence and a future should become a reality for some of the AIDS orphans and families of Rakai.

The team I went out with were going to assess and judge the five projects which had been shortlisted. The Rakai Branch

Project consisted of five income-generating activities. The winning branch would have the use of a four-wheel-drive vehicle for one year, which was a greatly sought-after prize. The judges' main aim was to ensure that the projects which had been submitted in writing were actually in situ and being run properly, also that the book-keeping was being done accurately. The purpose of the projects was to raise money to support the orphans and to train them in ongoing, income-generating activities which would result in their independence. The women had started the projects with small amounts of money and were then training the orphans and handing over the projects to them.

We went through the most wonderful fertile countryside on our way to the project sites. Often it was raining quite hard, and as we passed villages and communities we saw many people walking along the sides of the roads in the rain. It was three hours before we reached Kyotera in Rakai, and we went straight to an office where we met the local chairperson of the Rakai Branch. The office was just a square hut, for which they paid a rent of 1,000 Ugandan shillings (60 pence) per month.

Unfortunately our team had been expected to go the day before, stay overnight and start their inspection of the project at 8.00 a.m. When we arrived after 1.00 p.m. many of the people presenting projects, who had waited all morning, had disbanded so that they could go home to lunch.

In the hut where we met the chairperson, there were three sewing machines and the first project we saw was the tailoring project. The project had started with the purchase of two second-hand sewing machines. Three young girls (orphans) had been taught to sew and had gained a contract from a local school to make the school uniforms.

The judges spent some time talking to the executive committee of the region, led by Mrs Kagoa, and looked at all the book-keeping. We then visited the five projects. One was a project to raise chickens. A chicken house was being built from wattle and papyrus. Once this was completed, day-old chicks would be reared to three months and sold. From the proceeds a further batch of day-old chicks would be bought and income would thereby be generated. Pig-rearing formed another project. The women had started with two baby pigs costing 300 Ugandan shillings each (approximately 15 pence), and they had now bred and reared them, and had about a dozen pigs ready for market as well as a large sow with nine piglets. We also saw a ceramic project where people were being taught to make pottery. It was in the early stages and they were not very good at it yet. I shall not say any more about this project!

The fourth project we saw was a nursery school situated up on a hill, where they had built two small buildings of mud and wattle. One was the classroom with its little desks set out, and a short way down the hill were the buildings for toilet purposes. These were thatched huts with a few stones arranged round holes in the floor: one hut was for the children and there was one each for the male and female teachers. Unfortunately, due to the delay in starting the judging, we did not see the children at the nursery. They had sat at their little desks for some hours that morning waiting for the judges, but eventually had to go home.

The last project was one making bricks from clay. They were being fired out in the open air with heat coming from the bricks piled high around a central fire. When fired, the bricks would be sold or used to build houses.

After seeing these and other projects, we were taken to a village and given lunch at 6.00 p.m! At the end of the meal we went outside into the garden, where the village elders had been called together. There was music and dancing, and they taught us one of their dances and in response we taught them the 'hokey cokey'.

Whilst in Rakai, I was also invited to visit two people with AIDS. The first was a young girl who was very sick. The second was a lady I will never forget. She was standing at the door of a newly-built brick house. She told us that after the death of her husband she was determined that her children would have a future and that she would do everything she could before she died to ensure that they did. First she had undertaken to learn brick making, and she had made all the bricks used to build her house. With the help of other family members, she had then actually built her house. She took us to the courtyard, where we saw pullets that she was rearing from day-old chicks. She told us that when she sold them she was going to buy not only some more chicks, but she was also going into pig-rearing. What an inspiration she was to people who felt that once they were found to be HIV positive, their life was at an end. She told us that Jesus was her helper and had made all this possible.

There are numerous orphans in Rakai and in many cases, when both parents have died, the young families are looking after themselves, perhaps led by a girl of twelve years old and managing to stay together with the support of other women in the village. There are also many grandmothers, aunts and extended family members caring for the orphans. I saw one grandmother trying to care for seventeen children. But now it does not end there: the community itself, especially in the form of UWESO, are actively caring for the orphans in the villages, and these competition projects were another step in the right direction.

Despite the AIDS situation, Rakai did not seem to be a miserable, oppressed place. Certainly in the main shopping centres and streets, everybody was friendly and appeared to be happy, getting on with their lives. Even there, people were *living* with AIDS and contributing to the life of the community. I do not know the outcome of the project judging, but whether they are chosen to receive the prize vehicle or not at Rakai, they are certainly to be applauded for the efforts they are making for families affected by AIDS.

Now Mildmay was also going to be actively involved in helping AIDS sufferers in Uganda. It really was an amazing opportunity, an open field in which to develop our skills. It was wonderful to realise how carefully God had ensured that we would have the necessary opportunities to learn the things that we needed to know in order to develop Mildmay. The scholarships we had gained had enabled us to receive the necessary first-hand experience not only to develop appropriate services in London, but also to offer culturally sensitive training programmes that were acceptable in Africa. One thing had led to another in an extraordinary way: the study tour, the invitation to train, then the invitation to develop a centre in Uganda and the continuing expansion of international training opportunities. Over the last ten years, the pieces of the jigsaw puzzle had begun to fit together and we could start to understand God's purpose for some things which had not been clear earlier on.

Looking back and stepping forward

Now, finally, we come to Mildmay at the end of 1995 and the end of the book. Looking at a summary of our achievements over the last ten years, I have to say 'To God be the glory'.

- Mildmay was Europe's first and is now its largest palliative care centre for people with AIDS.
- Mildmay is now a provider unit to the National Health Service with 93 per cent of its revenue budget funded in that way.
- The main residential unit now comprises three wards and thirty-two beds. There is a suite where families can stay, and care is given by an interdisciplinary team of doctors, nurses, chaplains, counsellors, social workers, dietitians, physiotherapists, occupational therapists, a massage therapist and an art therapist.
- The Day Care Centre provides care for up to ten local people per day.
- The nursery cares for up to twenty children – ten outpatient and ten inpatient places – from 8.00 a.m. to 8.00 p.m., seven days a week. There is a clinical assessment for each child, and care is given by trained nursery nurses, a paediatric social worker, and a children's counsellor and bereavement counsellor. There is a waiting list for this service.
- The Family Care Centre cares for twelve families at any one time, enabling them to stay together when their time with each other is limited. 70 per cent of the patients are women on their own, 80 per cent of the patients are of African origin.

Care is given by the interdisciplinary team and this centre is a model of care, being the first of its kind in the world. Visitors from all over the world ask to visit it.

- The Centre for Advanced Studies has received recognition for the excellence of its education and training courses. It is a centre for post registration training for nurses, and health care professionals and students from all over the world also come for training.
- There are now three arms to Mildmay International.
  1. The consultancy service: people write, visit and telephone for clinical advice. The consultancy offered relates to the care of people with AIDS and their families, and to the setting up and development of services responsive to the particular needs of a country.
  2. Mildmay International AIDS Programme (MIAP): this is the training arm and provides training programmes for health care professionals and others related to care, management and counselling for people with AIDS, and the management of health care provision.
  3. The development and management of satellite units: e.g. Mildmay Uganda, a care, research and advanced study centre in Kampala. Having purchased the land for Mildmay Uganda and cleared and fenced the site, we are now awaiting confirmation of funding from the British Government (ODA).
- Mildmay is at present in a time of financial stability. We praise God for His provision for the work, because all of the £3.3 million capital costs for the Family Care Centre have been paid. Our inclusive budget in 1987 was £250,000 – it now stands at over £6.4 million.

With the growth and development of the work at Mildmay, we have encountered greatly increased responsibility, but my experience has been that God's promises are true when He says, 'My grace is sufficient for you' (2 Cor. 12:9 RSV) and, 'As your days, so shall your strength be' (Deut. 33:25 RSV). We testify to this as we work for Him at Mildmay.

So what is Mildmay in the mid-nineties? Mildmay's work is not confined to buildings. I believe it is the Spirit of God, working through individuals He has called to this work, to His glory and for the extension of His kingdom. We are still called, through Mildmay, 'to heal the sick and to diffuse simple gospel truths', although we use different words and methods from those used a century ago. God has called together those needed to do His work. Through His provision he has enabled Mildmay in 1995 to be recognised as a centre of excellence, with the reputation for providing high quality care, education and training. Now Mildmay also has international recognition and we have the chance to demonstrate God's love in many parts of the world. What a privilege is ours.

As we look to the future it is not only with gratitude to God, but also with confidence that what He has started, He will continue and see through to completion. We cannot know what He has in store for us, either as individuals or for His work through Mildmay, but we can certainly look forward to the years ahead with anticipation and excitement.

'There is a time for everything' – and for Mildmay, since its work was founded a hundred and forty years ago, it has been 'a time to care'.